Finding the Elusive
GOD

Wishing you God's
peace & blessings,

Paul Scanlon, O.P.

Finding the Elusive GOD

Fr. Paul Scanlon, O.P.

Our Sunday Visitor Publishing Division
Our Sunday Visitor, Inc.
Huntington, Indiana 46750

Señor, a los que tengan hambre, dales pan;
Y a nosotros que tenemos pan, danos hambre de ti.

Lord, give bread to those who hunger;
And to us who have bread, give us a hunger for You.

A MEXICAN BLESSING

CONTENTS

PREFACE   9

ACKNOWLEDGMENTS   13

LEARNING THE GAME   15
Chapter 1. Hide and Seek   17
Chapter 2. Not a Sparrow Falls   26
Chapter 3. God's Work of Art   34

DEVELOPING THE SKILLS   43
Chapter 4. Blessed Are the Poor in Spirit   45
Chapter 5. The Power of the Spirit   56
Chapter 6. Horse Manure   68
Chapter 7. Forgiveness   76
Chapter 8. Awareness   82
Chapter 9. Thirsting for God   93
Chapter 10. Gratefulness   100
Chapter 11. Don't Judge by Appearances   108

CELEBRATING DISCOVERY   115
Chapter 12. The Church as Community   117
Chapter 13. Rooted in Christ   127
Chapter 14. Wonder and Worship   136

LOST AND FOUND   145
Chapter 15. The Humility of God   147
Chapter 16. Through the Eyes of Compassion   153
Chapter 17. The Good Fisherman   161

EPILOGUE   169

NOTES   172

PREFACE

No image captures the reality of life more fully than that of the journey. The journeys of *The Odyssey*, *The Canterbury Tales*, and *The Divine Comedy* are just a few that exemplify the truth of this. The Old Testament is a journey that most powerfully speaks to us who search for God. Where would we be without the Exodus? How else could God have demonstrated so poignantly that "I will take you for my people and I will be your God" (Ex 6:7)?

Like a ragtag army, we journey together with the Lord, encouraging each other by sharing our faith. As night falls, like campers and earlier shepherds and wise men, we need to sit around the campfire and relive moments of joy and struggle, those epiphanies in which we saw the hand of God, the face of Christ. Nourished by these tales tellingly told, we bolster each other's spirits so that at early dawn we have the strength to continue on. I share these stories with you — moments logged in my faith journey — with the hope that in some way they may enable you to discern the Lord's presence during your own pilgrimage. Our God delights in the game of hide and seek. He leaves us clues on how to find Him; and if we get discouraged, He will sneak up on us and briefly manifest himself so that we will be re-energized to continue the search. Using as a bridge stories of persons and events that were important in my continuing with the game, we will reflect together on ways in which we might deepen our prayer and the living out of our faith in the community we call Church. Hopefully, you will find this an encouragement to continue your growth in being poor in spirit, pure in heart, and renewed in your love of Christ. Like any journey, like the journey of Mary and Joseph to Egypt with the child Jesus, we will experience exquisite moments of joy as well as times of hard sledding, but God is as surely with us as He was with the Hebrews as they plowed on to the promised land. These stories brought forth from the treasury of my ministry took place in many parts of the world. So that the various pit stops on my journey do not confuse you, it may be of help if I briefly trace out the circuitous path of my travels.

My priestly life has been fairly evenly divided between pastoral, educational, and leadership ministry. The first ten years were joyfully involved in parish ministry, particularly with the young. At the age of 36, however, I was elected provincial, that is, the religious superior of our west coast Dominican priests and brothers. Those were momentous years — the years of the seventies with their social revolutions and Pope John's exuberant *aggiornamento*.

My first growing awareness of a level of life, culture, and values different from my own began during those eight years as provincial. During that period, our province staffed a very large mission area — about the size of Rhode Island — in the southern state of Chiapas, Mexico. Every year for eight years I journeyed to this place of poverty and beauty to meet for several weeks with our mission team, a team made up of three priests, six religious women, a brother, four lay volunteers, and one hired doctor. Under the leadership of a great bishop, our missionaries dedicated their lives to the various native tribes who accounted for eighty percent of the population. I witnessed the suffering yet overpowering faith of these indigenous peoples. Those years opened my mind to a world of poverty and hardship that I had not experienced. I witnessed firsthand the unjust demeaning of the Indian people by the non-native population.

Not long after I completed my time as provincial, the Mexican *federales* forced our team out of the mission because the landowners were unhappy that our non-Mexican missionaries sided with the indigenous people. Our team challenged the reality that the natives were being treated as slaves on the very land they once owned. History was repeating itself. The first bishop of that area, Bartolomeo de las Casas, O.P. (1474-1566), was expelled for the same reason four centuries earlier. The Mexican Dominicans, however, had long wanted to resume their ministry in Chiapas, so we made an exchange. They took responsibility for the mission in southern Mexico and our province took over their parish in the extreme north of Mexico in Mexicali, Baja California. When my provincialate ended, I went there as pastor and stayed on some nine years.

Later, I was asked to be in charge of the religious formation of our seminarians in Oakland, California. Midway through this period, with my heart still fixed on the plight of the Hispanics, I made a visit to Central and South America with twenty other U.S. Dominicans also involved in religious formation. The purpose of the trip was to make us more aware of problems of injustice in the southern hemisphere, with the hope that this would be an eye opener for us and that, in turn, we would promote among our young men and women in formation the cause of the oppressed and poor.

Following those years I served in Los Angeles as pastor of a culturally mixed parish of Hispanic, Anglo, and Filipino cultures. Some of the episodes of this period are described in these pages. My trips to the Philippines were both as provincial and as friend of Fr. Leo Hofstee, O.P., who served forty years at the Tala Leprosarium.

More recently I served as pastor of Holy Family Cathedral in Anchorage, Alaska, a parish that caters to some extent to the natives and Eskimos. After being there a few years I was again asked to serve as the religious superior of our seminary in Oakland. Now that this responsibility has been cared for, I am packing my belongings to help out as a missionary in the Aleutians and share the life and faith of people who live so far removed from the comforts of the "lower forty-eight."

This crisscrossing of continents allowed me to discover a commonality in the outlook of those who live close to the land, whose lives are often negatively affected by modern technology and materialism. I discovered a beautiful simplicity of faith that could enrich those of us who have materially so much more than they. These mediations are meant, in an odd sense of irony, to be an offering to each of us from the treasures of the poor, God's "lowly" ones, of what they can teach us about life and death, suffering and joy, prayer and contemplation, and the manifold ways we can catch a glimpse of an at times slippery God.

ACKNOWLEDGMENTS

In a special way I would like to thank the parishioners of Nuestra Senora del Rosario, Mexicali, B.C., Mexico, for their faith and love that enriched my life and deepened my faith. Also, I am most appreciative of the loving support of the parishioners of St. Dominic's parish in Los Angeles, as well as the people of Holy Family Cathedral, Anchorage, and St. Christopher by the Sea, Unalaska.

Ministering with my Dominican sisters and brothers has always been a joy and a blessing. A special word of thanks to Dr. Leonard Doohan of Gonzaga University for opening my eyes to the beauty and nuances of God's word in the Scriptures, to Chuck Dahm, O.P., whose tours to Latin America transformed us all, and to Bill Dodds and Mike Dubruiel of Our Sunday Visitor for their help and encouragement to struggle on with my writing.

Finally, a grateful prayer of praise and love to a beloved mentor and friend, Fr. Fabian Parmisano, O.P., whose passion for writing and preaching have always been a special joy to us all. Hopefully he understands that in these humbling days of illness his example of faith has rung out as inspiringly as the preaching and teaching of his earlier days of glory.

Fr. Paul Scanlon, O.P.
Pentecost 2005

Learning the Game

CHAPTER I

Hide and Seek

A good number of years ago G.K. Chesterton imaginatively described the universe as the result of the bubbling over of the exuberant love between Father, Son, and Spirit. The three of them were having such fun together in that eternal time of glory that they decided to play this game called "creation." Each day, as together they watched the sun rise in the morning sky, reach its apogee and then display a marvelous array of oranges and reds as it settled comfortably into the sea, with a twinkle in His eye, the Father would gleefully cry out, "Do it again."

Let's nudge that fantasy a bit further. In our mind's eye we picture the Mighty Threesome in their effervescent joyfulness pull off a most glorious stunt — the creation of the human person. With relish they invite Adam and Eve to be the first tenants of this marvelous new world. But as happens so often in their future progeny, pride proves to be their Achilles' heel. Blinded by hubris they fall for the temptations of the wily serpent. In that moment of disobedience the tectonic plates of the earth become derailed and grind to a halt, the earth trembles and splits, rocks and rolls. The resultant tsunami comes roaring in from the great seas and all of creation is shattered and the garden destroyed.

But love is stronger than death, and the inventors are not easily disheartened. They pull out of their hat a new game called "hide and seek," a participative game in which those who can find their illusive creator are invited to take an active, cooperative part in shaping a new creation even more magnificent than the first attempt. It is agreed that at some historical juncture the Son will come and live among us, but disguised, so that only those with knowing hearts can discover Him. That discovery will bring such joy that the one who encounters and accepts Him will never be the same again. The irony is that the Son seems to play His role too well, for He fools more people than He may have intended.

> Though he was in the form of God, [he] did not count equality with God a thing to be grasped, but emptied himself, taking the form of a servant, being born in the likeness of men. And being found in human form, he humbled himself and became obedient unto death, even death on a cross (Phil 2:6-8).

Now you do have to admit that is a pretty clever disguise! Would you think this God you are looking for would let himself be battered and nailed to a cross, the most disgraceful form of death in His day? And so our God meets serious rejection. The four Gospels trace out which people were able to recognize this God in disguise and accept Him and which ones didn't recognize Him. Later generations are puzzled that it seems the wrong people emerge as the finders: sinners, the rejects of society, questionable ladies, and tax collectors.

How is it that we join the ranks of those discoverers? In the first prayer of the Church each morning, *Matins,* the very first psalm that is read to invite us to prayer, Psalm 95, repeats the phrase: "Oh that today you would hearken to his voice! Harden not your hearts, as at Meribah" (Ps 95:7-8). How often do we hear that voice? How well do we know how to listen or where to discern the hidden presence of God? Seeing and hearing are not easy skills to master. A person listening to classical music for the first time may well find it hard to appreciate, not knowing what to listen for. Another person watching their first football game will be puzzled by the intricacies and rules of the sport and find himself utterly bewildered. A counselor needs to not just understand what the counselee is saying, but listen for what is not being said.

When Jesus took Peter, James, and John to the mountain and was transfigured before them, they heard the voice of God saying: "This is my beloved Son, with whom I am well pleased; listen to him" (Mt 17:5). Have we learned the art of listening? Have we mastered the ability to see Christ transfigured in the simple events and ordinary people around us? Aren't there times we can identify with those that Jesus chided for having eyes but not seeing and having ears but not hearing (see Mk 8:18)? Are we like the children who come running when Mom calls, "Dinner's ready," but suddenly go deaf when she says, "Time to wash the dishes"? My hope is that as you read these pages you will pick up hints and skills in how you may more readily encounter this God who so enjoys playing hide and seek with us. And hopefully one day, that blessed day, you will discover Him in what we might think the least likely place of all — right there in your own heart and soul.

> **We come to recognize God's presence slowly by learning to read our feelings, desires, or even moods and behaviors.**
>
> — Sr. Sheryl Frances Chen

What is the secret insight, then, that allows some to find and accept Jesus and causes others to be blind and reject Him? We find the answer in Scripture. Mary herself gives us a clue as she speaks to Elizabeth: "For he has regarded the low estate of his handmaiden. For behold, henceforth all generations will call me blessed ... he has put down the mighty from their thrones, and exalted those of low degree" (Lk 1:48-52). "Those of low degree" are the *Anawim* of the Old Testament, a people humbled by the hardships of life, but by that very experience opened to the blessings of God. The Psalms and the prophets frequently speak of them. The prime example of "those of low degree" will take flesh in the person of Jesus, in that "he did not count equality with God a thing to be grasped" (Phil 2:6), but humbled himself accepting even death on a cross. What was accomplished by Jesus when He "emptied himself" is a basic principle of spiritual growth. We empty ourselves of our self-will so that God can fill us with His loving grace. In the case of Jesus, it was done voluntarily; in our case, God generally has to hammer it out of us. Those of low degree are the ones whose eyes and hearts have been opened by the vicissitudes of life.

They are generally of the poorer class. In the mind of the Hebrew, the poor are not so much economically poor, but powerless. The widow, the orphan, and the alien are the classic examples of persons whom the prophets are called to defend. Being powerless, they are naturally taken advantage of by the mighty and the rich. Thus, they hold a special place in God's heart. The rich and powerful are at times enslaved by their power and wealth, blinded to the goodness of God. Jesus advises us "unless you turn and become like children, you will never enter the kingdom of heaven" (Mt 18:3). Being childlike signifies powerlessness. It is an attitude, a state of being, that allows for openness, an openness that invites the power of God to come and fill the person with grace. "But to all who received him, who believed in his name, he gave power to become children of God" (Jn 1:12).

St. Thomas Aquinas writes that there are two ways to come to knowledge of God. One is by the use of reason, the other by way of connaturality, or we might say, "intuitively." That is, as in the case of the mystics, in the quietness of one's love one understands who the God of love is. The powerless, the simple, and the childlike relate to the suffering Christ, and in that are open in a special way to His grace and love. The compassion they develop helps them to relate to and understand a compassionate God, a good shepherd. The most important liturgical feasts in third world Mexico are not Christmas and Easter, but Ash Wednesday and Good Friday. For in most people's lives there is still a crucifixion and the people find a loving heart in the crucified Jesus.

Compassion gives us a greater depth of vision. I know a parish where a support group among Filipino parishioners was founded for parents of children who were disabled psychologically, emotionally, or physically. Once a year, these parents were asked to speak at Sunday Mass and share their experiences. They would speak of the excitement of having a new child and how much they loved it. But then one day they began to notice there was something different about their child, something out of balance. Gradually they became aware that indeed their child was "different." This sparked a long process of guilt, the thought that somehow it was their fault. Then came the temptation to blame the other person — it was the genes in the other person's bloodline that caused this. In time, with God's help they were able to work all this through and their marriage and family life became a blessing to them. A transformation, a new way of "seeing" had been experienced. Their child was no longer a "problem" child, but was the source of continued challenges and at the same time of continued impetus to growth. They discovered the face of Christ finely traced in this child. The result was a very compassionate love for others in pain, a reaching out to them, a bringing them closer to Christ.

Through our struggles and failures we come to a new depth of understanding of life, a deeper awareness of the presence of God, an ability to see Him disguised in the suffering and the poor. An opening of our hearts brings an opening of our eyes, a new perspective on life, new values. The lens of faith enables us to discover Christ present in all the simple events of daily life. Remember those moments in our lives when Christ came to us in countless disguises through people who one way or another strengthened us, comforted us, healed us, and challenged us by the power of Christ alive within them? It seems we all need to pass through some point of conversion, some struggle that, if endured well, does not lead us to bitterness but to a new ability to see, to discover a new depth to life, a new sense of love we had never dreamt possible. Like St. Paul we need to be

knocked off our horse and blinded so that we can find a new
way to perceive reality. As Abbe Huvelin puts it:

> To suffer with Christ is to be more extended in charity,
> it is to feel more the sufferings of others and to press
> them to the heart. The more one suffers, the more one
> understands that souls are, more than anything else,
> beings that suffer and that need to be consoled and
> relieved, rather than punished and corrected.[1]

We must not be discouraged by our weakness or our seeming ordinariness. Beethoven was deaf when he composed his
greatest works. Einstein was described by one of his teachers as
"mentally slow and adrift in his foolish dreams." Franklin Roo-
sevelt was crippled by polio. Abraham Lincoln failed in two
businesses, had a nervous breakdown, was rejected from law
school, lost four jobs and eight elections before he was elected
president, perhaps the greatest of our presidents. Could they all
not have joined in with St. Paul: "When I am weak, then I am
strong" (2 Cor 12:10)?

One of the great "seers" in Christianity was St. Augustine,
who fought God off for so many years, until finally, jolted by
the reading of a passage in Scripture, he was moved to change
totally the direction of his life. After surrendering to God he
speaks in the words of a new person:

> Late have I loved you, beauty so old and so new; late have
> I loved you. And see, you were within and I was in the
> external world and sought you there, and in my unlovely
> state I plunged into those lovely created things which you
> made. You were with me, and I was not with you.[2]

A fruitful discipline for exploring God's subtle presence in
our daily lives is the "Ignatian *examen* of consciousness." This
is not an examination of conscience such as in preparing for the
sacrament of reconciliation, but rather a discerning of how God
was active in your life today and how you responded to that pres-

ence. The process is to take a few minutes at the end of the day, recollect ourselves, begin with a brief prayer of thanksgiving, and pray for light to make our *examen* critical and penetrating. The area to probe is not just where and how did I experience God this day, but rather *what was my response* to God's seeming presence or absence. For example we could ask: What drew my attention to God today, what event, person, idea, scene, or episode, what feelings or emotions? What did I discover today about the way God works in my life? What enabled me to find the Lord in the difficult or painful experiences I had this day? Was I a sign of the Lord's presence to someone today? How was I aware of Christ in my work today? In what ways did I become aware today of my being loved, my sinfulness, my willingness or failure to respond? All of these are avenues we can take to reach a better understanding of where God is in our daily life and how we respond or blind ourselves to that presence.

One of the principles of St. Thomas Aquinas' teaching is that all we know comes to us through the senses. I believe we can amplify that and say that examining our emotions will teach us much about how we are relating to God. Our feelings help us to understand much about ourselves. For example, "Why do I feel jealous of this person?" What is the root of that jealousy, what is it in me that needs healing, what is the Lord trying to teach me as I discover this jealousy? As Sr. Sheryl Frances Chen suggests:

We come to recognize God's presence slowly by learning to read our feelings, desires, or even moods and behaviors. This knowing is primarily a heart-knowing before it is a head-knowing. This implies that we are in touch with our deeper, more enduring feelings; we can identify them accurately and own them. If we cannot do this, we shall more than likely act them out or blame them on others. Then they are lost on us, the very ones for whom they are intended.[3]

Without this reflective process of becoming conscious of God's elusive presence in the daily to and fro of life, we simply remain blind to these little epiphanies and could well own those words of Augustine: "You were with me, and I was not with you." Let us join together in being explorers and discoverers, work together to open the eyes of our hearts and find the presence of God subtly hidden in every nook and cranny of our lives. Let us recapture the sense of mystery and awe we had as children first discovering the sights and sounds of that magic world out there, a simplicity that was tarnished as we grew older and developed a sophomoric conceitedness. Honed by the winds of life's humbling experiences, let us recover and refine that purity of heart and arrive at a more mature and balanced virtue of childlikeness. Chesterton uses the metaphor of the person who grew so bored and irritated by the smoke-filled skies, contamination, and crowdedness of London that he set sail to discover new, brighter worlds. After some time sailing about in foggy weather he comes upon new land and moving ashore discovered the glorious excitement of a new city, bustling with people, buildings reaching to the sky, smells of delicious pies and pastries filling the air. Then it was he realized he had sailed in circles and rediscovered London, seen it with new eyes, recovered lost beauty. May we see the world through the keen eyes of Gospel vision.

> Then turning to the disciples he said privately, "Blessed are the eyes which see what you see! For I tell you that many prophets and kings desired to see what you see, and did not see it, and to hear what you hear, and did not hear it" (Lk 10:23-24).

I watched in awe as the small, sinewy native brought his wife to our jungle hospital. He had physically carried her for three days down the Chiapas mountain paths. She was tied seated, facing backwards, onto a rugged wooden chair that was fastened around his back. He was bone weary by now. She was critical with tuberculosis. In this sacrificial love for his wife he had honored Jesus — "As you did it to one of the least of these my brethren, you did it to me" (Mt 25:40). Here in the jungle mountains I witnessed an epiphany, God made visible in this act of love. This Tzeltal native was the good shepherd, literally carrying the lost sheep on his shoulders. The impact was very powerful, for it was at the same time a love beyond what his culture demanded. I had become accustomed to see the native families file into town. First came the man, carrying nothing but his machete in his hand, occasionally flicking a weed or bit of brush out of his way. Some three paces behind came the wife. Like a beast of burden she balanced on her head a large pot of water, draped over her back a bundle of firewood, and in the front a baby tied in such a way that it could nurse whenever the need struck her. This humble gesture of the native husband to be the beast of burden for his wife was Christ-like. Whenever we see such love, we see the face of God.

QUESTIONS FOR REFLECTION:

1. What are some of the persons, places, and events in my life that have been special manifestations of or encounters with God in my life?

2. Which of my feelings, moods, goals, or behaviors indicate my closeness to or distance from God?

3. What do I understand St. Paul to say in the phrase: "When I am weak, then I am strong" (2 Cor 12:10)?

4. When I was moved with compassion for someone, what new perspective on life did I experience? In what way did I experience Jesus in my reaching out to another?

CHAPTER 2

Not a Sparrow Falls[4]

The tropical rain pounded the sixteenth-century church so hard it was nearly impossible for us to hear one another, a great excuse to take a break from our staff meeting. My fellow Chiapas missionary team members and I stepped outside, stood under the eaves, and chatted idly until we noticed an indigenous man standing in the cloister garden.

He had no umbrella, no rain gear. Apparently beaten down by more than the storm — perhaps even unaware of the foul weather — he didn't move. I wish I could say I rushed over to help him, but I didn't. Another team member, Sister Mari, stepped out into the rain and led him inside. She dried him off. Fluent in Tzeltal, she listened to his story.

His name was Manuel. His wife had just died, and he didn't know what to do or where to go. We agreed that Sister Mari would accompany him to the carpenter's shop and have a casket made while the rest of us went back inside the church to continue our meeting.

That evening after dinner, Sister Mari and I, accompanied by Fr. Vincent, the pastor, headed out in the mission's truck to pick up the grieving widower and the coffin. We loaded the simple pine box into the truck bed, and then Manuel and I climbed in beside it. By now the storm had passed through Ocosingo and was headed toward Guatemala, but the road was thick with mud as we drove off beyond the edge of town and past the last few houses and their faint lights.

Manuel told us when to stop. It wasn't just in the middle of nowhere; it was in the middle of a pitch-black, sloppy, muddy nowhere. We slid the box out and began our trek to Manuel's house. He and Sister Mari, holding a flashlight, led the way. Fr. Vincent and I carried the coffin, hoisting it above our heads as we crossed through a deep culvert filled with rushing water. Then, after climbing up the other side, we crossed a field in pure blackness except for the flashlight's faint beam.

After a couple hundred yards, Manuel told us to stop. We had arrived. He lived in the field. His house, his home, made of sugar cane and pine branches woven together, had no lights, no driveway, no address. As the beam of the flashlight splashed against the tiny structure, I could see a small opening in the curved roof and a wisp of smoke. The house had no chimney.

Fr. Vincent and I got down on our knees to shove the box inside. We eased it alongside the body of Manuel's wife, which was lying on the wet earth in the one-room hut. A small fire was burning on the floor. It was mostly a handful of embers, but the occasional flicker of flame showed that the woman had been in her mid-thirties. I can't tell you her name; I never learned it.

With difficulty, Fr. Vincent and I lifted her to place her in the casket. Not accustomed to this kind of face-to-face encounter with a dead body, I was startled by the gurgling of fluids as we lowered her into the box. As the pastor began to slide one end of the coffin lid toward me, a young boy slipped between us. I hadn't seen him in the semidarkness; my attention had been fixed upon the dead woman.

The young son was saying goodbye to his mother. He gently straightened out the woman's hair, wiped the moisture and bits of mud from her face, and kissed her on the forehead. No one moved as he took a *petate* — a light bedroll — and laid it over her in a simple but profound gesture of love and farewell. Fr. Vincent and I resumed positioning the lid and used rocks from the field to pound the nails into place. We later learned that on the following day, prisoners from a nearby jail were escorted out to the field to dig a grave and bury her.

That evening was a sacred moment for me. That mud floor, I'm certain, was holy ground. Even today I remain touched by the tenderness with which the boy caressed his mother's face in one last gesture of love. I remain moved by this young woman's slipping away from this world so quietly.

Since that evening, I've been comforted by the thought that although she was a stranger to even the people who lived in Ocosingo, she was known and loved by God. Since that evening, I have thought of that bedroll; I have remembered that box. Years later, I served as a pastor in Los Angeles and attended or presided at many burials at some of the most exclusive cemeteries in the world, the final resting place for some of the world's most famous people.

But even as I stood in those lush settings, surrounded by extremely ornate statuary, my mind returned to that field in Mexico. My hand again felt the rock I had used to pound those nails. Not a sparrow falls from the tree without the Father's knowing it, Jesus told us. That little sparrow — that wife, that mother, that woman whose name I never heard — *is* known and loved by God. He cherishes her. She is wrapped in a *petate* of infinite love.

Your name defines you, denotes your special identity, and roots you in time and place. Have you ever had the experience of being in the airport picking someone up or waiting to be met by another person? The bustling about of thousands of people and the raucous flow of announcements over the public address system surround you like flotsam and jetsam on a rushing river as you anxiously look about for a familiar face. Suddenly, as though surging up from your unconscious, your name is announced over the speaker, and despite your previous inattention to all the other names spewing forth, hearing your name aloud hits you like a bolt of lightning. Someone is hoping to find you, and this being called by name gives you a sense of joy, a sense of being found. "I once was lost, but now am found."

More than giving us a personal identity, our Christian name reminds us that we belong to a family, that we are neither alone nor adrift in this vast world. Unfortunately, we seem to be losing the lovely custom of giving our children a Christian name. That name given to us at baptism reminds us that we belong to the family of God, that we are the living temples of the Holy Spirit, and that we have been given a patron saint to guide and protect us in our journey through life. We are not alone. We are more than citizens of a particular nation or state, we are citizens of the kingdom of God. That is what gives us special dignity and beauty.

In many cultures the given name defines the person. "Chrysostom" means "golden tongued," a quality for which St. John Chrysostom was known because of his great preaching. In the book of Genesis, Jacob, after wrestling with an angel, had his name changed to Israel because he had "striven with God and with men, and have prevailed." Jacob then named that place Peniel, "For I have seen God face to face, and yet my life is preserved" (Gen 32:30). In the New Testament, Saul's name was changed to Paul and Simon's name to Peter, indicating their new being in life as followers of Christ.

> **More than giving us a personal identity, our Christian name reminds us that we belong to a family, that we are neither alone nor adrift in this vast world.**

A name can also signify power, as in calling someone "Governor" or "President." At the Last Supper, Jesus tells the disciples that if they ask anything of the Father in His *name*, He will give it to them (see Jn 16:23-24). Peter heals a cripple saying, "I have no silver and gold, but I give you what I have; in the *name* of Jesus Christ of Nazareth, walk" (Acts 3:6, emphasis added).

Right there at the beginning of the commandments given to Moses we read: "You shall not take the *name* of the LORD, your God, in vain" (Ex 20:7, Deut 5:11, emphasis added). There is in fallen humanity that iconoclastic quirk in our nature that wants to strike out and smash the sacred, graffiti the beautiful. And so when frustrated and angry we ridicule the name of God or deride the beauty of sexual intimacy. In doing that we are demeaning ourselves. If we make something ugly of the God who created us, we are making junk of ourselves. Isn't it much more beautiful to honor Christ with reverence, as St. Paul urges us in his letter to the Philippians, "that at the *name* of Jesus every knee should bow, in heaven and on earth and under the earth" (Phil 2:10, emphasis added). The Father has given us life and the Son has restored that life. In honoring them we honor ourselves as well, recalling that it was out of love and for love that they created us. The more we understand who God is, the more we understand the beauty of who we are — temples of the Holy Spirit.

God, who has knit us together in our mothers' wombs, knows each of us by our most intimate name. In Isaiah we read: "'Can a woman forget her sucking child, that she should have no compassion on the son of her womb?' Even these may forget, yet I will not forget you. Behold, I have graven you on the palms of my hands" (Is 49:15). His love for each of us is unique as the creator carefully crafts us by hand leading us along labyrinthine pathways known only to a loving God. No one is nameless, no one is an orphan, each of us has our name written on the palms of God's hands and inscribed on Jesus' sacred heart. In some divinely gifted way, God knows each of us in our distinct uniqueness, for as we are reminded in Psalm 139: "Thou knowest when I sit down and when I rise up; thou discernest my thoughts from afar . . . For thou didst form my inward parts, thou didst knit me together in my mother's womb" (Ps 139:2, 13); or, as Isaiah says, "The LORD called me from the womb, from the body of my mother he named my name" (Is 49:1).

It is in finding God that we find our true self, and conversely it is in finding our true self that we find God. We will see later that, as Merton says, the journey to God is a journey inward. It is a journey of discovery, a growing awareness of the Godhead dwelling in our deepest self that gives us identity, meaning, and joy. In the 18th chapter of Genesis, we read that elderly Abraham and Sarah are visited by three men and in that meeting experience an encounter with God. Abraham offers them hospitality, shares with them his home. They in turn offer him a gift of life. They promise that within a year this elderly, barren couple will have a longed-for child, Isaac, and through Isaac Abraham will be the father of many nations, the father in faith of those whom we now know as Jewish, Christian, and Moslem. So too if we offer hospitality to God we will find Him dwelling within us as the source of life and fruitfulness. St. Catherine of Siena encourages us to "know thyself," for in doing so we discover our innate hunger for God, our call to be His family. Our God is a God who seeks us with love, a Shakespearean suitor who relishes in wooing our hearts. We are all part of God's flock, each of us will be received with tenderness and wrapped in God's arms as was the prodigal son, as was this humble woman who lived in a field.

The unborn that go unnamed present another matter for reflection. Not infrequently, a woman will approach a confessor, very contrite and burdened because sometime in her life she had an abortion and is still haunted with hurt and guilt. It may have been because the father was unprepared for such a responsibility or her parents put great pressure on her, or her own poor judgment may have led her to this decision. As Jesus did in the case of the woman caught in adultery, we must condemn the sin but love the sinner. I have found the advice of an older and wiser confessor to be of help in restoring hope and healing to such a mother. I suggest that she *choose a name* to give her deceased child, to accept ownership for the child she once rejected, for the child is indeed alive and close to God. The *Catechism of the Catholic Church* states:

> Indeed, the great mercy of God who desires that all men should be saved, and Jesus' tenderness toward children which caused him to say: "Let the children come to me,

do not hinder them" (Mk 10:14; cf. 1 Tim 2:4), allow us to hope that there is a way of salvation for children who have died without Baptism" (CCC 1261).

The *Catechism* no longer makes any mention of Limbo.

The love, the anxiousness, in the mother's heart for her aborted child is a love that God placed in her. God could not put this love in her if His love for her child were not even greater than her own love. In the mother's love for her child, she is experiencing a faint reflection of God's far greater love for the child. Even more awesome is that this transformation from guilt to a freer and fuller love of her family is the evidence of God drawing good out of evil, using as leverage the memory of her own child who has become a source of sanctifying grace for her. It is inconceivable that God would use an innocent child as the source of grace and sanctification of another human being without that child participating fully in the graces granted. The amazing reality, then, is that this unwanted child becomes, through God's kindness, the instrument of the mother's sanctification. What does the child want more than to forgive her, sanctify her, and be the source of blessings on the family she never got to enjoy but looks forward to sharing with in the fullness of eternal life? The growth of the mother's love for her other children and for her husband are evidence of the child's intercession on their behalf. This is the special mission that God intended for the infant when He first granted it the gift of life in the mother's womb. Just as the Holy Innocents played their role in God's plan of salvation, so this innocent child is a special saint and intercessor for her family. The mother's love for the child then becomes a place of discovery, of encounter with a loving God. Wherever we find love, we find something of God. And so even this painful moment can be made an epiphany of God's marvelous presence.

There are times when it is hard for us to accept forgiveness, believing that what we have done was unforgivable. We could not be more mistaken. There is nothing more that our loving God wants than that we be lifted of that burden, so that we can more fully live the life God has given us. Like Lazarus, God wants us to rise from the dead here and now and get on with life. We do neither our neighbors nor ourselves any good if we live like zombies, frozen in our guilt. I remind these women, myself, and all of us who at times feel entombed in guilt, of the beautiful words of the prophet Micah: "Who is a God like thee, pardoning iniquity and passing over transgression for the remnant of his inheritance? He does not retain his anger for ever, because he delights in steadfast love. He will again have compassion upon us; he will tread our iniquities under foot. Thou wilt cast all our sins into the depths of the sea" (Mic 7:18-19). Off the coast of Monterey, California, there is a canyon in the sea deeper than that of the Grand Canyon. Perhaps it is there that all our sins have been tossed. Those shipwrecks no longer exist in the mind of God.

QUESTIONS FOR REFLECTION:

1. Jesus' name means "Emmanuel" — "God is with us." In what ways does this name define our God and make Him different than the pagan gods of the Old Testament or other pre-Christian cultures?

2. My name indicates my God-given uniqueness. What are some of those qualities that I see that identify me, that mark out my uniqueness?

3. My baptismal name defines me as a member of God's family. How has that affected the way I live out my life and the goals I have set?

4. Within a year after his wife's death, Manuel also died. His son, named Petúl, was adopted by a young Mexican-American couple who served as lay volunteers at the mission. What qualities of God's personality do I see reflected in this action?

CHAPTER 3

God's Work of Art[5]

It was 120 degrees in the shade. A normal summer day for Mexicali, a sleepy Mexican village south of the California border that had burst its seams and now numbers over a million people. Farmers irrigate with the dregs of the Colorado River, foreign businesses string out their sweatshops along the barbed-wire barrier that divides two countries, two very distinct cultures.

We were gathered around in an arid open field where I had folded out the card table that would serve as our altar. "Please, Father, come and say Mass for us," the women had begged repeatedly, until I finally yielded. I came one Sunday afternoon a month. The teenagers I had brought from the parish strummed away on their guitars leading the assembled families in practicing a few hymns for Mass. The air I inhaled baked my throat. The dust from the field clogged my nose. A blazing sun charbroiled us.

I stood in the dry weeds a few feet away hearing confessions face to face with these humble people who were as hardened by life as was the adobe with which they baked their bricks. Giggling boys would admit having put frogs in their mothers' bed or a garter snake in their sisters' dress. Men would own up to drunkenness and beating their wives and children. Poverty had beaten them down, made them feel useless. They were forced to live in cardboard and plywood houses because their *patron* paid them so little they couldn't afford to use the very bricks they baked.

A sprinkling of about thirty families lived in this field where they baked bricks from the adobe soil on which they lived. No air conditioning. No running water. Few trees. They shared with each other whenever someone lacked food or clothing. They always offered us *frijoles* and enchiladas. Juanita would slice off a stout leaf from the cactus growing next to her house and prepare it for us to eat, chopped up and boiled, filled with vitamins.

La Ladriellera, "The Brickyard" was a mission within a mission. I invited a few adults and some youth from our nearby parish to accompany me each month to bring clothes, song, and friendship to these humble people on the edge of society, an invitation to be Jesus to His beloved poor. It gave joy and meaning, indeed, to our parishioners. But was it demeaning to the poor? Did it only make them feel castoffs to receive castaway clothes? Could they see the sincerity that motivated their visitors?

Each Sunday that I shared with them the Scriptures I struggled to find something to say that would bring them hope. What would Jesus tell them? As I read aloud the words of Mass, I sometimes wondered if they thought I was speaking a language from outer space. The theological nuances and niceties would have been lost on them. Did they somehow sense Jesus' presence? Did they grasp that just as the helpless babe was present in that grungy feed trough in Bethlehem, that same Jesus was present now in this dry, thirsty field to offer them living water? Did they comprehend that they were as welcome as the first grubby shepherds? What to say to them?

The answer struck me one May 3rd, the Mexican date for the feast of the Holy Cross, the patronal feast of carpenters and bricklayers. Driving by a building under construction, I spotted a large wooden cross that had been hastily fastened on the structure by the workers. The words of St. Paul flashed through my mind: "You have been purchased at a great price" (1 Cor 6:20; 7:23). Jesus had stretched out His arms to embrace us, to call us to be His brothers and sisters, to be His family. Just as Francis gave dignity to the leper by his kiss, so Jesus gives us acceptance and dignity by purchasing us at the cost of His very blood, sharing our lives, inviting us to share His life in turn.

"You always have the poor with you" (Mt 26:11; Mk 14:7), Jesus said. Which one of us is not poor? Which one of us does not hunger for love, acceptance, and worth? Who has not experienced moments of self-doubt, been crushed by feelings of worthlessness? In the competitive American society in which we live there is so much pressure to win, to succeed, to be popular. Failure is a terrible disgrace: failure at marriage, loss of a home, being fired from work, a debilitating illness. All are devastating. Sexual abuse, marital bashing, poverty, all erode away a sense of worth and dignity. It is because of His own experience of rejection, of what seemed like "total failure," hanging there naked on the cross, that Jesus becomes the epitome of compassion. Long before the Bishops of Latin America made a "preferential option for the poor," Jesus had chosen the humble of the earth to share in the riches of His love. He is always at our side in those dreadful moments of life to remind us that we are indeed loved, that we are His family. Royal blood flows in our veins.

Crucial to spiritual growth is the acceptance of this truth — we are God's beloved. Why do we reject this love as did Peter: "Depart from me, for I am a sinful man, O Lord" (Lk 5:8). Is it because we fear it will call us to a true conversion of life and we aren't up to the task? Why do we blind ourselves to the dignity and beauty that God has poured into us? Is it that we cannot admit to ourselves that we are loveable? Years of hearing confessions, spiritual direction, and pastoral ministry have revealed to me that there is in us a strong sense of guilt, of self-dislike: "Lord I am not worthy." Why do we hide from the God who seeks us? Jesus' desire is to call us forth from this tomb as He did Lazarus, to free us from our fears, self-doubt, self-pity, that we might grow and blossom for His glory. If we think we are but junk, we will behave like junk. If we realize we are loved, we will give life to one another. We will treat each other and ourselves with the dignity all deserve.

No one is junk, even if, as some of my former parishioners, they live in junk yards. You are fashioned by the tender hands of God. The Artist who had crafted Orion and the Pleiades, the Grand Canyon and Yosemite Park, fashions each of us with love and skill. When we can accept that, say "yes" to that, we are at the dawn of new birth, new life.

⤳

Approximately thirty years ago, a Mexican priest founded a movement for lower class laborers: field workers, carpenters, bricklayers, men who sell tacos and popsicles on the street. Men whose lives are a bit like the crucifixion. He called the movement *La Escuela de la Cruz* — "The School of the Cross." The first requirement for entering was participating in a weekend retreat spent in very humble quarters: a large wooden building without fans to lessen the burning desert heat, sharing sleeping space on the floor with hungry cockroaches. Before the retreat began the men were herded together outside the front entrance, and the person directing the retreat would begin by insisting that this retreat was only for "*macho*" men. "Would those who are *macho* raise your hands?" he hollered. Bewildered, only a few hands would go up. The director would repeat several times, "This retreat is not for sissies, only real men, *macho* men," until finally everyone raised their hands boasting they indeed were tough *hombres*.

As the retreat began, however, he would start to work his magic as he shifted gears and commenced to ridicule this attitude. "Yes, isn't it great that you are all *macho*, that you beat your wives and chase other women? Isn't it great that you are so brave and strong that you beat up your children and drink until you cannot find your way home? Isn't it great that you are so courageous, so manly?" Bit by bit he would lead them to see that real strength lies not in domineering and selfish egotism, but in loving, humble service of others, the humble service that a courageous Jesus embraced on the cross. Lives were changed, families were blessed, and communities were enriched, as these men discovered the treasure of Jesus' love and courage. They realized that it takes great courage to live our faith in today's secular atmosphere. These simple men, men like the earlier fishermen and tax collectors, heard his call that they be his Apostles of today, that they embrace the cross with that courage and pride that runs deep in their Mexican blood.

The crucifix is our sign of hope. An ancient Christian motto claims, *Crux est mundi medicina* — "the cross is the world's medicine." The Church boldly displays it in full view to call our attention to two great truths. First, that we have been bought at a great price, that we are deeply loved, loved even in our sinfulness. Jesus chose the Apostles right where they were, rough edges and all. Living daily in his presence, their lives, values, and attitudes began to change. They began to shed their selfishness and pride like withered leaves and replace them with the new foliage of compassion and generosity. Jesus is not turned off because of our sins or weaknesses, for He knows better than we the potential for good and strength that lies dormant deep down in our souls. To be awakened to growth, all the seeds need is acceptance and openness on our part to the magical touch of the Spirit so that they might rise from their slumber and flower for the glory of God and the refreshing renewal of our Christian community.

> He who hung the earth in its place hangs there; he who fixed the heavens is fixed there, he who made all things fast is made fast upon the tree.
>
> — Melito of Sardis

Secondly, it takes two beams to make a cross: one vertical, one horizontal. The vertical one symbolizes the love between God and ourselves, our humble reaching up to a loving God who pours down upon us His love, not for us to hoard for ourselves, but so that we can stretch out our arms horizontally and share that love with our sisters and brothers. The cross is a beautiful reminder of the two great commandments folded into one — love of God and love of neighbor. One cannot exist without the other. Love is always a call to sacrifice, a total giving, of which the cross is the supreme symbol. The cross is not just what happened to Jesus — it is who He is. "We preach Christ crucified" (1 Cor 1:23), Paul declares. The God whom we worship is a crucified God.

For this reason, the Church boldly displays not just a cross, but also a crucifixion, a body battered and beaten, hanging on that wooden frame. It is not because we don't believe that Christ in His one supreme sacrifice has not risen and gone to the Father. Rather it reminds us that in some way the crucifixion still continues. While Saul was persecuting the early Christians, Jesus appeared to him and asked, "Saul, Saul, why do you persecute me?" (Acts 9:4). The risen Jesus has identified with the persecuted Christian community as though it were His very body. As Paul points out so many times after his conversion, Jesus is the head and we are the body. When we suffer, Jesus is there sharing the cross with us.

The crucifixion continues everywhere there is poverty and hunger, every time there is war and violence. Jesus is always with the downtrodden, the weary, those who suffer injustices, the victims of abuse. How can He not be there, for after all He has loved us enough to give His last heartbeat for us, and like a good shepherd He never abandons us. So, in some odd, difficult to understand sense, the crucifixion goes on. St. Paul possibly had that in mind when he said, "Now I rejoice in my sufferings for your sake, and in my flesh I complete what is lacking in Christ's afflictions for the sake of his body, that is, the church" (Col 1:24). We are always encouraged to unite our prayers, sacrifices, and sufferings with the heart of Jesus in His concern for the wounded of the world. A most important way to find our God is precisely in our neighbor, Christ in me reaching out to Christ in my sisters and brothers: Jesus teaches us: "Truly I say to you, as you did it to one of the least of these my brethren, you did it to me"(Mt 25:40).

The name of the game that the Mighty Threesome challenge us to play is "Finding and Being Found." Hopefully, the next chapters will aid you in this discovery. Wisely recalling that, as we look, we keep in mind the words of the Creator of the game,

"For my thoughts are not your thoughts, neither are your ways my ways" (Is 55:8). That's what makes the game tricky and not easy to learn.

A haunting story has come down from the holocaust period. The Nazis, supposedly for some act of disobedience, were hanging a number of prisoners while the other prisoners were forced to watch, to burn into their minds what would happen if they didn't follow the rules. Among the men was a young boy so frail and light that when their bodies dropped from the scaffolding he hung there gasping and dying slowly, for his weight had not been enough to break his neck. A taunting whisper came from one of the observers, "Where is your God now?" A prisoner replied, "He is hanging there in front of us." Whenever we suffer, Jesus suffers. We do not suffer alone, though, for as the letter to the Hebrews states; "Because he himself has suffered and been tempted, he is able to help those who are being tempted" (Heb 2:18).

> He who hung the earth in its place hangs there; he who fixed the heavens is fixed there, he who made all things fast is made fast upon the tree ... (Melito of Sardis, 2nd century preacher).

QUESTIONS FOR REFLECTION:

1. What is there in my deepest heart that makes it hard to accept the fact that God loves me so deeply? What do I hesitate to give up or do in order to be more open to this love?

2. "It takes more courage to be compassionate than to be a bully." Why is that so?

3. At what moments in my life did I experience meeting Jesus, feel His eyes look lovingly upon me, sense His calling me by name?

4. Can I list areas, such as racism or prejudice, where I have found it difficult to treat persons with the dignity they deserve?

Developing the Skills

CHAPTER 4

Blessed Are the Poor in Spirit

The "poor in spirit" is an awkward phrase that easily could be misinterpreted as indicating a lethargic person, one with no "get up and go" — someone demoralized or lacking in spunk. In reality, though, it means just the opposite — a person whose love for God is straight as an arrow, right to the heart. He or she is a person energized by the Holy Spirit, uncluttered with mixed motives, uncompromising in their purity of intention. I know many persons whom I would consider fine portraits of "poor in spirit," but I know well that I cannot claim that qualifier for myself. There's too much in me yet of the "false self," the need for approval, the desire for success, the craving to look good in the eyes of others, the attempt to be something I am not. Becoming poor in spirit, however, is one of the ways of perfecting our ability to see God.

At the deepest level, to be poor in spirit is the same as to be pure of heart. The one whose heart is pure is also the one whose spirit is unencumbered by anything that would distract it from a total love of God. Someone poor in spirit is indeed very rich, because she has no need for anything other than God. Or, perhaps better said, the presence of God in her fills her so completely that in all she meets, does, and possesses, God is fully there. Her love is so pure that she is forgetful of self. St. Francis is a good portrait of one who is poor in spirit when he says in his beautiful prayer, "O Divine Master, grant that I may not so much seek to be consoled as to console; to be understood as to understand; to be loved as to love." No need there of approval or praise — just a desire to give of oneself and let love be its own reward.

"Blessed are the poor in spirit," Christ tells us, "for theirs is the kingdom of heaven" (Mt 5:3). The one who is poor in spirit has a total freedom of spirit. He has freed himself from the need of all passing things, is unattached, non-possessive, because his only wish is to be possessed by God. His longing heart comes to God with a total openness. It does not put obstacles in the way. It brings the emptiness of its poverty before the overwhelming generosity of God. Like air rushing into a vacuum, God fills the heart that has emptied itself out for Him and is always ready to receive more love and more light. Poverty is the door of blessedness because Christ chose poverty in that "he did not count equality with God a thing to be grasped" (Phil 2:6) but poured out His life to fill our empty vessel with divine life. "For you know the grace of our Lord Jesus Christ, that though he was rich, yet for your sake he became poor, so that by his poverty you might become rich" (2 Cor 8:9).

In these pages I offer examples of persons who were materially poor, who, through their struggles, became indeed living icons of the poor in spirit. There are many who are not nearly as economically poor but who also could be described as poor in spirit for they are not attached to or possessed by their material goods. However, it is important to remember that it is not just material goods that we must not be attached to. We must also not be attached to such things as false self-images of ourselves or even to our spiritual blessings. St. John of the Cross writes a good bit about the difficulty it is for some religious people to not cling to the spiritual consolations God has given them, to beware of not loving the consolations of God, but rather the God of consolations.

The process of arriving at purity of heart and poverty of spirit may well be a long, difficult one. Like the magi we are led on by the shining star of faith, seeking the fullness of love in Christ, but find that the journey is long and wearisome. As in T.S. Eliot's poem, "Animula," we all start out as innocent children: "Issues from the hand of God, the simple soul." But then we launch into a search for success, fame, and power that make of us complicated, divided persons, "... irresolute and selfish, misshapen, lame, unable to fare forward or retreat."[6] But, with God's grace and life's grinding burdens we hopefully return to a long lost simplicity of heart. However, it will require some deliberate choices on our part to opt for a simpler life style. When Jesus was led by the Spirit into the desert and was tempted, He made some specific choices. He purposely chose not to be a Messiah of pomp and military power, but a servant Messiah opting to identify with the poor and outcast. If we want to be a close follower of Jesus we too must opt for a simpler life style, for example, a choice of less extravagant possessions, aware that our possessions often end up possessing us, enslaving us with their demands. As a family we can decide on less television time, using that spare time for healthier family activities, for shared reading, for centering prayer — a practice many husbands and wives have adopted. We could even opt for choices of food and drink that reflect our desire to have our entire life humbly ordered to God.

I remember a lovely little film the Franciscans put out some years ago. I don't remember the title or even the purpose of the film, but etched deep in my mind's memory I have sketched the scene. The setting is in an "old folks home." There, in a rather spartan recreation space, about a dozen elderly folks are seated in their wheel chairs in a semi-circle. All are bent over, their minds wandering down the corridors of old memories, sad, lonely, some drooling, others nodding off. Awkwardly, trippingly, a small young girl, a toddler about two years old enters and stands there in their midst. Ever so gently each of the elderly persons becomes aware of her lovely presence, their heads and shoulders gradually elevate, and joyful warm smiles shine forth from their face like the sun peeking through after a long storm, the warmth of joy scrunched up over them like an old favorite blanket. The innocence and simplicity of the young child encounters the childlikeness of time-tried souls. After years of wandering and harsh north winds, these weary old pilgrims had recaptured that early innocence, now matured like rich wine. "Unless you turn and become like children, you will never enter the kingdom of heaven" (Mt 18:3). They were ready, it struck me, freed enough in spirit, to move on home to the Lord in joy.

The poor in spirit come in various sizes and shapes, much like the lovely old bottles that could be found in an apothecary shop or in modern-day garage sales. For example, a parishioner who is a recovering alcoholic, a tough former marine, and a Vietnam vet. First thing every day he reads over the daily Scripture readings for Mass, and probably due to a faith deepened by that prayerful *lectio divina* he also is a volunteer fireman and medical emergency response person, despite the fact that his regular workday is twelve hours. Another parishioner, who has that rare gift of waking up every day as cheerful as eggs sunny side up, gave up his work as a car salesman, at which he was very successful, to dedicate himself to managing a full-time job as director of a feed-in center ministering primarily to struggling Eskimos. He begins the day serving the early morning Mass.

> **For you know the grace of our Lord Jesus Christ, that though he was rich, yet for your sake he became poor, so that by his poverty you might become rich.**
>
> — 2 Cor 8:9

I have a friend, mother of three, whom the neighbors call "Mother Teresa" because she is always reaching out to the down and out. I admired her for asking her children to wait table on the street people who came to the Sunday pancake breakfast, to show them some kindness, even though some parishioners wanted me to show them the door because they smelled and looked so bad. I have petitioned the diocese to award the annual St. Francis Medal to a catechist who has served the parish for twenty-five years with love, energy, and creativity, despite the fact she has a serious vision impairment. In my forty-five years of ministry I have seen many such persons, from the Guatemala border to the Aleutian Islands, that define by the quality of their hearts better than I can in my own words the example of the poor in spirit, the pure of heart.

I also would like to speak a word of encouragement to those who are the "water boys" of the Christian community. I was an only child, spoiled in many ways, underprivileged in others. I didn't have siblings with whom to fight and argue, and therefore I grew up meek and mild and to this day greatly dislike acerbic disputes and confrontation. So, even though I wasn't a clumsy ox as an athlete, I wasn't adept at being competitive and feisty. Worse still, in high school I had a horrendous problem with acne that not only negated any social life with young ladies but also made it impossible for me to wear shoulder pads and play football. So I signed on as water boy for the football team. At time-outs during the various games I would rush in with fresh water and encouraging words to keep the real boys, the stars, buoyed up and raring to go.

As I grew up I shed the acne but the scars of sensitivity and insecurity remained. I always felt more comfortable doing "the dirty work" around the parish: the manual labor, the work of organization. Even as a pastor and later as provincial I felt more comfortable with the simpler people than with high society, more at ease with the blue collar crowd than with intellectually astute and sophisticated leaders. As I will relate later (in chapter 12), I once tried playing the role of prophet, of promoting the cause of social justice, but, overwhelmed by peoples' rebuffs, I slunk away from that form of ministry. A Daniel Berrigan I am not.

It was, however, the poor and humble class of Mexicali that gifted me with their wisdom that one need not be a bishop or governor to be beloved by God, for these men who sold tacos on the street and the women who worked picking lettuce under a broiling sun were as Christ-like as anyone I ever met in the sacred halls of the Vatican. I am greatly indebted to these humble people so rich in faith and generously accepting in their love.

I am sure the gigantic redwood tree relishes its grandeur, but there is just as much beauty and artistry in the delicate daffodils that live at the foot of the tree. God wisely created a variety of trees and flowers, of people and animals, for if everyone were a gigantic sequoia the scenery would be monotonous. Each of us has our role to play. Each of us, as St. Paul so well reminds us, has our gifts and charisms. Henri Nouwen comments: "Spiritual greatness has nothing to do with being greater than others. It has everything to do with being as great as each of us can be. True sanctity is precisely drinking our own cup and trusting that by thus fully claiming our own, irreplaceable journey, we can become a source of hope for many."[7]

Only recently, while visiting a parish where I had served, a man came up to me and said, "Father, I know you don't remember me, but some years ago I came to you for confession and the words you offered me gave me hope and changed my whole life." I was humbled. Just a simple water boy helping the Lord, unbeknownst to me I was able to bring hope and joy to this person so that he could turn his life around. I have wondered at times if the patron saint of water boys could possibly be the unknown person that offered Christ vinegary wine on a sponge stuck on a reed of hyssop. Recall that hyssop was used by the Hebrews in their flight from Egypt to sprinkle the blood of the sacrificial lamb on their doorposts so the angel would "pass over" their house and slay only the first born of the Egyptians. John's gospel plays on this symbolism, as Fr. Raymond Brown points out: "When Jesus drinks the wine from the sponge put on *hyssop*, symbolically He is playing the scriptural role of the paschal lamb predicted at the beginning of His career, and so has finished the commitment made when the Word became flesh."[8] So when this anonymous water boy holds up the hyssop with the wine on it Jesus completes His work, the greatest and most difficult task undertaken by anyone, and can triumphantly say, "It is finished," bow His head, and hand over the Holy Spirit (Jn 19:30). Maybe when we feel we're not the stars of the show, but simply part of the scenery, we can remember how this important role in fulfilling the Scripture and our salvation was played by a person whose name and fate no one knows but God alone.

Perhaps you can glimpse the way in which poverty of spirit and purity of heart are one and the same thing. Poverty of spirit is only another aspect of the purity that wants nothing but love; that will allow nothing to get in its way, not even itself, before the infinite outpouring of divine love. It is like lovely glass through which light pours undistorted and undimmed, without deflecting the smallest ray by any imperfection. But like the glass, the person who is pure in heart has gone through his own fires and shaping. The crucible of suffering — of love, prayer and reflection, conversion and transformation — through which the Holy Spirit has led it, has finally brought the soul to a sense of peace and simplicity. The soul is now free, has moved from a false sense of self to an awareness that "it is no longer I who live, but Christ who lives in me." The heart of God was its furnace of transformation. It was the fulfillment of the promise of God through Ezekiel:

> I will sprinkle clean water upon you, and you shall be clean from all your uncleanesses, and from all your idols I will cleanse you. A new heart I will give you, and a new spirit I will put within you; and I will take out of your flesh the heart of stone and give you a heart of flesh. And I will put my spirit within you, and cause you to walk in my statutes and be careful to observe my ordinances . . . and you shall be my people and I will be your God (Ezek 36:25-28).

An anonymous Carthusian reminds us that maybe God loves the poor in spirit so much because that is precisely the definition of our God: "Each Person (of the Trinity) is fully himself through the gift of himself to the others. Their fullness is in their poverty; they are not diminished by their self-emptying."[9]

The task of supervising the formation of a purity of heart is delegated to none other than the Holy Spirit. The Spirit has a large box of tools to accomplish this change of heart, among which we find three very important surgical tools: love, suffering, and prayer. Here let me say just a brief word about prayer. Many are the shapes of prayer: prayer of petition, adoration, praise, recitation of the rosary, centering prayer, *lectio divina*, prayer using images such as in the spiritual exercises of St. Ignatius, and prayer beyond thoughts. With what I suppose is a bit of presumption, I would like to offer a simple style of prayer that embraces all of them and is rooted in the Christian tradition from the desert hermits as well as modes of prayer popular today. Having spent many years trying on for size all of the various forms of prayer as mentioned above, I have found an approach that I propose to those of us, either lay, clerical, or religious, who find ourselves so busy, the former raising a family, the latter overburdened with excessive apostolic ministry due to the present shortage of priests, brothers, and sisters.

I recently proposed the following model to the parishioners in Unalaska ("Dutch Harbor") in the Aleutian Islands. The people who work in the canneries there during the ten months of the various fishing seasons work a minimum of 12 hours a day, six or seven days a week. Often they work eighteen hours a day. How can they find the time or the energy to spend much time in prayer? The ideal for centering prayer is half an hour twice a day. As deeply as I love centering prayer, it is unrealistic of me to ask that of people in the fishing industry. So the method I propose can be adapted to your daily schedule and can be abbreviated or extended as the day allows. It can be adapted to centering prayer, the Rosary, the spiritual exercises of St. Ignatius. It is basically in the pattern of *lectio divina,* that is, a prayerful reading of Scripture. The only adaptation I propose is to translate the four steps of *lectio divina* into English in an alliterative way of facilitating an easy mnemonic device to recall the four steps.

Let's call it **"the method of the four R's"**:

1. **Read**
2. **Reflect**
3. **Respond**
4. **Rest**

Read: Select a passage of Scripture. As a beginning exercise, pick a passage from the gospels that involves some action, such as Jesus inviting Zacchaeus to come down from the tree and accompany Jesus to his house. Or perhaps Jesus calling Peter to leave his boat and follow Him. Read the passage slowly, savoring it as a sparrow savors each drop of water, not guzzling it, but relishing it as we would a fine wine.

Reflect: As in the Ignatian method, situate yourself in the scene. Drink in the sights and sounds of the scene, letting yourself be part of that memorable moment. For example, in reading the story of the wise men following the star, imagine the cold of night, the hardships of the journey, the sense of excitement as they draw near their mysterious goal. Legend has it that the author of Luke's gospel was possibly a medical doctor. Notice how throughout his gospel Luke, as an observant doctor, makes us aware of the emotions of the personages: Jesus "rejoiced" (Lk 10:21), "had compassion" (Lk 7:13), "wept" (Lk 19:41), and "marveled" (Lk 7:9); or the people "marveled" (Lk 11:14), "were astonished" (Lk 4:32), and "were filled with awe" (Lk 5:26). Be like Luke in your observations of the mood, the tension or peace of the moment, the surroundings, and the various personalities.

Respond: Let your heart speak from what you experience. "Lord, like the wise men I anxiously seek to find you. Lord, at times I get weary of the journey, I find myself tempted to search for other goals; I find that I am lost or frightened." Let whatever is in your heart well up and speak to the Lord.

Rest: Just be quietly present to and with the Lord, like when you have climbed a hill and come to an overlook that lets the beauty of nature startlingly reveal itself to you. Without any words, just drink in the beauty of God. "Be still, and know that I am God" (Ps 46:10). If you find yourself distracted, just quietly — as in centering prayer — gently say inwardly your sacred word, or for a brief moment reflect on your breathing as you feel the air being inhaled and exhaled through your nostrils.

The twelfth century Carthusian, Guigo II, describes the stages of this form of prayer: "Reading carries food to the mouth, meditation chews it and digests it, prayer extracts its flavor, and contemplation is the sweetness itself that gladdens and refreshes."[10] This approach can be used for a fifteen-minute space of prayer, or as an introduction into your time of centering prayer.

As in a drama, the beginning and ending are important moments. Begin by taking a moment to quiet yourself down, to recollect yourself. Go into the hermitage of your heart where Christ is always present, awaiting you. Close the doors of your imagination and daydreams. Ask Mary or your guardian angel to keep that door closed during your time of prayer, and then launch out into your prayer with Jesus. At the end of your available time of prayer, slowly recite an Our Father to ease yourself back into the activity of the day.

May Mary, who "kept all these things in her heart" (Lk 2:51), lead us to her son, Jesus. May she who is purest of heart, fullest in Spirit, be our daily partner in prayer.

QUESTIONS FOR REFLECTION:

I. Jesus was born poor, raised in humble circumstances, identified greatly with those marginalized and heavily burdened. What effect does this aspect of His life have on the lifestyle choices I make?

2. Which simple, "ordinary" people have I met in my life that indeed have opened my eyes and enabled me to see Christ present in them?

3. How am I able to live a "simpler life" in a culture that puts such emphasis on luxury, success, and fame?

4. Relationships wither if there is not time for being together. What are some possible ways for me to find time for a simple, quiet moment of prayer with the Lord?

CHAPTER 5

The Power of the Spirit

Seated in the very last row of the second-class bus, I was sand-wiched between two Bolivian women wearing those odd round English Bowler hats we have all seen in issues of the *National Geographic* magazines. Twenty other Dominican sisters, brothers, and priests were scattered throughout the bus as we bounced and jiggled our way along the Andean plateau from the city of Oruro to the world's largest silver mine four hours distant. We were on a six-week tour of Latin American countries to observe first hand the problems of injustice and third world poverty.

The Andean plateau, over 12,000 feet in altitude, does not support tree life, only shrubs for the alpaca and llama herds to graze on. Bolivia is a land-locked country. In an 1879-1884 war with Chile it lost its seacoast and as a result has no port from which to export its own rich minerals and products. Consequently it is the second poorest country in Latin America, second only to Haiti.

Two hours through the journey one of the women seated next to me pried herself loose with the purpose of speaking to the driver. With her native hoop skirt bulging out and covering her legs and feet, she floated down the aisle of the swaying bus like a skiff bobbing along the surface of the sea. Promptly the bus came to a halt on the dirt road and most of the natives unloaded to relieve themselves in the fields. We Americans were too inhibited to join them and prayed we could hold it in until we reached our destination. The native women, however, needed only to squat a few feet from the bus, as years of experience had taught them the usefulness of these long hoop dresses that clothed them like a tent and served as the Andean version of the "porta-potty."

At length we arrived at the silver mine that we were to tour, guided by Oblate missionaries. As I gazed about at the lunar landscape a twang of conscience made me feel a bit guilty that I was not doing such heroic work as these Canadian missionaries. Looking around at the barren mountain that sheltered in its womb the precious silver, the desolate scraps of housing, and the lonely remoteness of this place, I was convinced that these missionaries should be canonized just on the sheer merit of living there.

After a brief introduction and history, we entered the mine's opening at an altitude of 12,000 feet. Along with the workers, we climbed aboard and squatted down on small railroad flatcars. Being taller than the average 5-foot 6-inch Bolivian male, I had to take seriously the warning to keep my head down or be fried, for the high voltage wires that powered the train were only about six inches above me. The Oblate priest that accompanied us related that the workers were paid so little that while working in the mine they would chew on the cocoa leaf to abate their hunger. The workers did not receive enough salary to provide sufficient food for themselves to make it through the day without this drug that eased their hunger pangs. Yet they worked in the very bowels of the world's richest silver mine! Every few years the native workers would revolt and attempt a strike for higher wages. The response was always the same. The government would send in soldiers, and the workers would either return to work or face getting shot.

Caught in this dilemma, the workers attempted to find strength and support in their faith. During our tour, the Oblates took us up a crude elevator to the second floor and into a Catholic chapel that had been excavated alongside one of the tunnels. Next, we went to the first level and into a small room with a statue of "Pachamama," the goddess of the earth and fertility. The voluptuous statue was adorned with cocoa leaves and incense. The workers were hedging their bets and cautiously pleading with both the pagan and Christian gods for alleviation from their misery and safety in this dangerous mining operation.

I recalled stories of my uncle and cousins who had spent their lives working the coal mines of Pennsylvania, stories of the tyranny of the company store, tales of them working on their bellies in caves only three feet in height, clumsily attempting to swing their pick ax and dislodge chunks of coal from the earth. The great John L. Lewis was their savior, as he summoned up the courage to unionize the men and eventually bring about some reform for safety and better working conditions for the miners. The cause of justice and human dignity is as ancient as the Old Testament prophets. Prophets like that are still needed. It is a challenge that Jesus holds out to us today.

"If you want peace, work for justice," said Pope Paul VI, a frail but courageous man. I am not good at being heroic. I like to think of myself as compassionate. But is that my way of dodging the bullets of the battle to defend the dignity of the human person? Am I a draft dodger in the skirmishes against racism, abortion, the death penalty, materialism, and all that snuffs out the torch of human dignity?

In a very real way we are each a precious mine filled with the raw materials of spiritual wealth and power. There is richness in us greater than the silver mines of Bolivia or the diamond mines of South Africa. In the very heart of our mine lives the Holy Spirit, who, with His fire, is burning away the dross and purifying that gold and silver to a brilliant beauty (see Is 48:10). As we cooperate with the Spirit and let Him chip away the impurities of fear and self-centeredness, the riches of God's powerful love may burst forth from our deepest depths to heal a world hungering for peace and justice. Those precious jewels are the multifaceted beauty and power of the Christ-like virtues that facilitate us to be supple instruments in the hands of the Spirit and act with wisdom, strength, and compassion. Some may be called to speak boldly, others more softly. Some will be called to protest courageously, others to visit the poor and the lonely, to sacrifice their time and interest for the sake of their family, or simply to befriend their neighbor. What marvels can be accomplished if we bring forth those gifts to enrich the society in which we live.

> My son, if you come forward to serve the Lord, prepare yourself for temptation. Set your heart right and be steadfast, and do not be hasty in time of calamity. Cleave to him and do not depart, that you may be honored at the end of your life. Accept whatever is brought upon you, and in changes that humble you be patient. For gold is tested in the fire, and acceptable men in the furnace of humiliation. Trust in him, and he will help you; make your ways straight, and hope in him (Sir 2:1-6).

Life is about power. We enter the world totally powerless, helpless babes in our mothers' arms. As we grow, we struggle to move away from that power, with varying degrees of success. Ideally, we need to be empowered by our parents so that we may be able to leave the nest with a healthy balance of maturity. As the blessing ceremony for a fifteen-year-old Mexican girl reads: "To grow is to mature, and to mature means to accept responsibilities and fulfill them." This moving away, however, is a wrestling match, not just with our parents, but with ourselves, determining which direction we should go to search for and use our power. Some will be tempted to seek it in silver and gold, fame and success; others will consider sharing that power in service, sacrifice, and creativity. So there is a tension, which St. Paul describes so well in his writings, between the power of the Spirit and the power of the flesh, the flesh here meaning the darker side of human nature, such as selfishness, greed, and violence.

We must be careful not to see the world as evil, for in Genesis when God finished all of creation He saw that "it was very good" (Gen 1:31). And indeed it is. Yet, as in the loveliness of the desert in bloom, there are snakes and scorpions that could waylay and overcome us. The call of the Spirit-filled person is to cooperate with God in the redeeming and beautifying of the world.

We read also in Genesis that when God created the first human, Adam, He breathed life into him. The word for "spirit" in the Bible means precisely that: "breath." Therefore when we speak of "spirituality" we are speaking of deepening the life of the Spirit within us, of being empowered by the very breath of God. The Spirit is diaphanous, transparent, and translucent. The Spirit can only be seen indirectly. For example, we all seem to perceive the face of the Spirit in the grace filled life of Mother Teresa. We can see the Spirit active in the life and ministry of Jesus, which in turn enlightens us on how the Spirit touches our lives. Jesus was not baptized because He was burdened with original sin, but rather that the power of the Spirit be made visible in how He lived and carried out His ministry. To know how the Spirit might work in us, we could not find a better source for reflection than the writings of St. Paul and the ministry of Jesus, especially as described in Luke's Gospel. In just one chapter of Luke we see the Spirit descend like a dove over Jesus at His baptism, the Spirit then leads Him to the desert to be tempted. Having passed that test, the Spirit leads Jesus back to Galilee where He teaches in the synagogues and finally returns to His home town of Nazareth, where in the synagogue He reads from the book of Isaiah proclaiming that the passage being read is here and now being fulfilled precisely because "The Spirit of the Lord is upon me" (Lk 4:18). As Fr. John Haughey, S.J., points out: "The Spirit did not teach Jesus higher math or physics or existentialism. He taught Him who He was."[11]

Jesus himself warns that there is serious tension between the power of the world and the power of the Spirit. Paul forcefully spells out that difference. "Now the works of the flesh are plain: immorality, impurity, licentiousness, idolatry, sorcery, enmity, strife, jealousy, anger, selfishness, dissension, party spirit, envy, drunkenness, carousing, and the like" (Gal 5:19-21). Quite a laundry list, isn't it? "But the fruit of the Spirit is love, joy, peace, patience, kindness, goodness, faithfulness, gentleness, self-control" (Gal 5:22-23).

The danger of worldly power is that we feel we don't need God. We're doing well enough on our own, thank you. But eventually the powerful will be humbled. When we think we are powerful is when we are actually the most vulnerable. "But God said to him, 'Fool! This night your soul is required of you; and the things you have prepared, whose will they be?'" (Lk 12:20).

Numerous times while hiking in the Sierra mountains I would be amazed, observing a small green twig of pine forcing its way through a tiny crack in a rock of solid granite. As years would go by that power for life would force the mighty rock apart as the tree grew thicker in size. Life will not easily be put down. Each of us has that kind of power, even though we may well be unaware of it. A smile can make a person's day; a frown may make a child wither. A compliment can encourage more responsible behavior; a harsh word may destroy a person's self-confidence. We have much power in our use of words, gestures, and deeds. Our prayer must be that they are always life-giving.

Worldly power has as its goal that of making us successful, comfortable, and secure. The power of the Spirit is to shape us that we be givers of life. "Peacocks today, feather dusters tomorrow" is a popular saying. The world encourages us to be peacocks, to preen and strut; Jesus prefers we be feather dusters, to be of service one to another. Worldly power, then, means an active forcefulness of personality, whereas the power of the Spirit is only gained by surrender, by admitting our weakness. The Lord replied to St. Paul, "My grace is sufficient for you, for my power is made perfect in weakness" (2 Cor 12:9). Emptying out, *kenosis,* is a principle of spiritual growth, being emptied out of our egocentricity so we can be filled with God. It is not an easy task, and so we often shun it. "Let go and let God" is a slogan of both the AA groups and the medieval mystic, Meister Eckhart. Or, as other saints frequently repeat, "God cannot fill us up until we have emptied ourselves out." Scripture tells us, "Unless a grain of wheat falls into the earth and dies, it remains alone; but if it dies, it bears much fruit" (Jn 12:24). The tension, then, between worldly power and spiritual power is that the former has a compulsion for ever more power, whereas spiritual power is a greater letting go. In that act of letting go is precisely where we open ourselves to the enormous power of God, of love, of creativity, of joy and peace beyond measure. That surrender, as was that of Jesus' final surrender on the cross, is the point of breaking through, of obtaining the golden key to the real, true kingdom.

> **In a very real sense we are each a precious mine filled with the raw materials of spiritual wealth and power.**

Fr. Rolheiser explains that "to let God be God means to undergo the presence of God as a tree undergoes the presence of summer. The metaphor is extraordinarily simple: a tree is brought to bloom by summer. It does not capture summer, understand summer, conceptualize summer, nor is it even able to project what summer will do to it."[12] It simply surrenders to its life-giving power.

We are all familiar with the powerful figure of Abraham and how in his old age he was called by God to slay his own son, Isaac, even though Isaac was the only hope Abraham and Sarah had of seeing fulfilled God's promise that their progeny would be greater than the number of stars in the sky. As Abraham is in the act of obeying God unquestioningly, God, moved by his obedience, relents and lets Isaac go free. We all have our own Isaacs to slay before we can really be free to follow God fully. Isaac might be our pride, our greed, or our ambition. I look back on my life as a priest and realize that, although I worked so hard and faithfully in my ministry, I now see I did much of it for my glory and not the Lord's. I can see how much I enjoyed the power of leadership, the adulation received for running a

well-organized province or parish. With a sense of shame I can
see that I loved it when people praised my preaching, but that
I was envious when they praised even more a visiting preacher.
Only after being humbled by failures or disappointments, or
being knocked off our horse, or a moment of grace, can we see
the Isaac in us we are called upon to slay. Humility is the first
step into wisdom, into a greater clarity of vision.

Unless we become like children — that is, powerless — we
are unable to enter the kingdom of God. Kathleen Norris points
out "that the grace of childhood lies in being receptive. And to
receive as a little child is to receive fully, with an open mind and
with gratitude for the seemingly limitless nourishment that has
come our way."[13] On the other hand, as Jesus says, the rich and
the worldly powerful will find this business of being poor in
spirit, of being God-focused, as painful as a camel squeezing his
way through the eye of a needle. Not that it is impossible.
Wealthy Joseph of Arimithea showed a humbleness of heart in
offering his own grave as a burial place for the crucified Jesus.
The patron saint of one of our biggest cities, St. Louis, was king
of France.

In C.S. Lewis's *The Chronicles of Narnia*, the children find in
the inner recesses of their bedroom closet a hidden door, a secret
door that when opened allows them entry to a whole new marvelous kingdom. Jesus repeatedly tells us that only the humble of
heart, the poor in spirit, the childlike will be able to fit through
the narrow door, will be given the golden key to this kingdom.
When we put our hopes in purely worldly treasure and power we
will discover that we have chosen the wrong kingdom, that we
were the big fish, but in the wrong pond. Our only way out of
this dilemma is a turning around, a conversion of heart, a becoming truly poor in spirit. Conversion is a process, ongoing, never a
finished product. A Buddhist monk states: "Here is a most exquisite paradox: As soon as you give it all up you can have it all. As
long as you want power you can't have it. The minute you don't
want power you'll have more than you ever dreamed possible."[14]

Several of us once went to visit a glass-blowing factory in Ciudad Juarez, just across the border from El Paso, Texas. We watched as the craftsmen skillfully spun their objects of art from the malleable molten glass. Each had a blow pipe some three or four feet in length. They would dip one end into an ingot of molten glass and lift up a fistful of the soft, hot semi-liquid material. Then blowing into the mass, with the other hand they would begin to shape a lovely figure — a rose, small elephant, or other attractive trinket. If it weren't coming out as they wished, they would toss it back into the ingot and begin again. With similar dexterity the Holy Spirit works to make something beautiful of us. And, if we are malleable and open, the Spirit can make of us something beautiful for God.

The Spirit then is the hidden treasure in our hearts which empowers us to come alive, to discover the panoply of ways in which God manifests himself, and the fashion in which we too make that presence visible. "If the Spirit of him who raised Jesus from the dead dwells in you, he who raised Christ Jesus from the dead will give life to your mortal bodies also through his Spirit who dwells in you" (Rom 8:11). This is a powerful statement. The very one who raised Jesus from the dead dwells and is at work at the very core of our being. Whenever we love, pray, are courageous and self-sacrificing, it is because we are fueled by the power of that very Spirit. As we enter into the quietness of our soul, the deepest interior of our ground of being, our hearts and prayers are caught in the upward draught of the flaming Spirit and swept up to the Father.

> Likewise the Spirit helps us in our weakness; for we do not know how to pray as we ought, but the Spirit himself intercedes for us with sighs too deep for words. And he who searches the hearts of men knows what is the mind of the Spirit, because the Spirit intercedes for the saints according to the will of God (Rom 8:26-27).

Deepening our life in the Spirit is accomplished through prayer, fasting, sacrifice, simplifying our lives, focusing more fully on the goodness of the Lord. It is not so much in great accomplishments that we honor God and make Him known, but even more fully in radiating the love of the Spirit, in being transparent vessels in which the Spirit's life is visible. Spiritual growth is not so much a greater effort on our part as though we were lifting weights to develop a stronger body. Rather it is being more aware of the life-giving presence of the Spirit at the core of our being and allowing that Spirit to grow from within us, like the flower that billows forth from the stock and slowly opens itself to offer its beauty to God and bask in His warm love. It is a kind of getting out of the way, a clearing of the ground around the bush so it can grow more heartily on its own power. In a sense, our growing in virtue is precisely that, a clearing away of the stubble and rocks, for the virtuous life gives us an inner freedom, a healthier environment that allows for a fuller growth of the Spirit from within us. However, that growth requires patience and trust. A seed only flourishes by being left in the ground to mature. If we keep digging the seed up to check whether it is growing, it will never bear fruit. Fr. Henri Nouwen advises:

> Think about yourself as a little seed planted in rich soil. All you have to do is stay there and trust that the soil contains everything you need to grow. This growth takes place even when you do not feel it. Be quiet, acknowledge your powerlessness, and have faith that one day you will know how much you have received.[15]

The greatest Spirit-filled person was the mother of Jesus, precisely because she was so wholeheartedly open to the power of the Spirit.

In recent years there has been an evolution in the style of delivering funeral eulogies that has resulted in a genre that is rather chatty and folksy, and not totally to my liking. For example, eulogists will relate such adventures as the time the deceased shot his first bear or she was the homecoming queen at the local high school. Nice pleasantries that would draw a chuckle or two. But then I thought, as Peggy Lee used to sing, "Is that all there is?" Isn't a person's life more than that? Tell us about her real life, her life with God, what coursed through her heart and filled her with fire and passion. In a sense, that deepest part of our life is like an underground stream, hard for us to plumb and measure. But isn't that the truest side of who we are? That is the side of us that breaks through in our actions, our choice of values, our compassion, our family life. Those are the shoots that burst forth from that part of us that is rooted in the God within us. The tree will be known by its fruits, and so that intimate relationship we have with God will flesh itself out in the quality of our being and the richness of our fruit. That's what we must focus on when we reflect on a person's life.

In the deepest recesses of our soul the Spirit of God breathes on the embers of our love and transforms us, that we be a living flame of love, that we have the courage to live our faith boldly and be concerned for justice and peace, that we hunger not just for the consolations of God but for His challenges that we be other Christs in the neighborhoods and marketplaces of the world. We are the temples of the Holy Spirit of God, a treasure far greater than all the gold and silver the world could offer. Let us be lighthouses for those who seek for God; let the light of the Spirit shine forth from within us that they may find their way back to the safe harbor of Christ in some humble way aglow within us.

Reporters asked Boris Yeltsin who it was that encouraged him to remain firm in the fight against communism in the former Soviet Union. Yeltsin replied: "I owe it all to a Polish electrician named Lech Walesa. When they asked Lech Walesa who had inspired him in his struggle, he said that it had been the movement for civil rights of the blacks in the United States which was begun and directed by the Protestant minister Martin Luther King, Jr. In an interview, Martin Luther King, Jr., affirmed that the strength of his inspiration was due to the courage of a simple black woman, Rosa Parks, who simply refused to sit in the rear seats of the bus, which was the section designated for the blacks."[16]

One simple person, empowered by the Spirit of God, can display for us the marvelous deeds and multifarious ways in which the Lord makes himself present to us.

QUESTIONS FOR REFLECTION:

1. How have I experienced the workings of the Holy Spirit in my life? In what ways may I be hindering the transforming work the Spirit is trying to accomplish within me?

2. What are the spiritual gifts God has given me? How might I develop them and with whom am I called to share them?

3. Who have been the formative persons of my growth in the Spirit?

4. In what ways may I have neglected concern for social justice issues, such as the death penalty, treatment of prisoners, racism, the marginalized, abortion, and treatment of the elderly?

CHAPTER 6

Horse Manure

Juanita sliced a tender leaf off the prickly pear cactus and with dexterity born of experience, scraped off the cactus needles, chopped up the large leaf into string bean sized chunks, and put them on the fire to boil. The youth I had brought with me from the parish were playing games with the youngsters who called these humble plywood shacks home. While waiting for Juanita to finish the meal, her young husband showed me how they made the bricks that was their livelihood. It is a simple, time-proven process. The adobe soil on which we stood is shoveled out and mixed with sand and the last dregs of the Colorado River that is shunted by an irrigation canal through their field. The muddy mixture is scooped up and shaped in a wooden mold and laid out like large cookies to dry under the broiling sun. After that the dried bricks themselves are used to form an oven about 12 feet tall and 12-feet by 12-feet square. The inside would be filled with firewood, lit, and burn for twenty-four hours.

With a smile he said, "But there's a secret ingredient added to the mixture so that the bricks don't just crumble." He pointed to a pile of horse manure. The partly digested straw gives fabric to bind the bricks, and some type of chemical reaction caused by the baking of the manure laced adobe gives the final product sufficient strength to be used for construction.

Now, isn't that true of life as well? It's the horse manure of life that makes us strong! Those misfortunes that come our way, or those problems that we bring on ourselves are the fires that test our mettle. The illnesses and tragedies that shake us to the core can be, ironically, what move us to change our lives, to center our hearts on God. As God advises us through His prophet Isaiah, "Behold, I have refined you, but not like silver; I have tried you in the furnace of affliction" (Is 48:10).

"Why me, Lord?" Haven't we all moaned when crises come crashing down upon us? Why does God allow terrorist bombings, the innumerable horrors of war, terrible natural disasters? We have no answer for that. We can only look at the crucifix and reflect that if God endured that for us, somehow He will be with us in those horrendous moments. There are valleys of darkness in our lives when we have to soldier on as best we can, doing our best to acknowledge that Jesus is there with us sharing the yoke of sorrow. Those are the moments in which we might push ourselves to reflect on Mary at the foot of the cross. Who would have thought it would have ended this way? Already, she had been bewildered by the mysterious words of the angel of the annunciation and struggled through the difficult circumstances of her son's birth — so far from home, no sanitized medical clinic in which to bring to the light of day the light of the world. She had observed Him grow as any other lad, yet with a deeper wisdom and more vibrant faith than the neighbors' children. In the course of years she watched from the corner of her heart's eye as He grew in wisdom, age, and grace before God and neighbor. Now, as her fully matured son accompanies her to the wedding at Cana, her faith in Him fully rooted, as a tree yields its ripe fruit the mother nudges her son — somewhat to His surprise — into His public career. "Do whatever he tells you" (Jn 2:5), she whispers to the stewards.

Was she regretting that now, feeling guilty and remorseful for having started Him unwittingly on the road that led to this dreadful hill? Couldn't she, of all people, have protested as she wept there on Calvary: "Why me? Why my son?" Since the fall of our first parents, the human race has been asking the same question: "Why me? Why my family?" And there is no answer. The whole book of Job was written to resolve this problem, and

Job's only answer was: "The LORD gave and the LORD has taken away; blessed be the name of the LORD" (Job 1:21).

Why is it that God dumps all these problems on us? Some Christians believe it is because they have done something wrong and God is punishing them. That's not the kind of God I want to believe in! Some non-Christians think it is a result of bad karma, that we're paying back for something we did wrong in a previous form of existence. The problem with that is we have no way of even guessing what, when, or where it was that we did something so evil as to deserve this punishment. Most Christians believe all is out of whack because of Adam and Eve. Others believe that, no matter whose fault it is, the horse manure of life can be used to our advantage, for spiritual growth.

The difficulty, of course, is that pain, tragedy, and loss can make us bitter. I know a woman who would complain that she was angry with God for the death of her husband. When I asked how long ago her husband had died, she replied: "Twenty years ago." A long time to drag that anchor around one's neck! People have committed suicide or become alcoholics because the pain was too much. God wields a dangerous weapon when He hauls out of His tool chest suffering as a crow bar to pry some growth out of us.

Yet, when we enter the church, what is the first thing that catches our eye but that big, huge crucifix hanging over the altar. In Mexico, Spain, and Italy, those crucifixes are really gory — blood all over, hair hanging loose, a body contorted in agony. The message comes through loud and clear. We have no reason to complain. "You were bought with a price" (1 Cor 6:20). Spiritual writers frequently encourage us to share our sufferings with Jesus to bring about healing and forgiveness. "By his wounds you have been healed" (1 Pet 2:24). Likewise, in our woundedness we can offer healing to others.

To suffer with Christ is to reach out in charity, it is to understand more fully the sufferings of others and to press them to the heart. The more one experiences suffering, the more one identifies with the other who needs consolation and strength. As St. Luke recommends, "Be merciful, even as your Father is merciful" (Lk 6:36). The merciful, compassionate person is a source of life and power, of joyful enthusiasm and energy. The humble Jesus always stands with the suffering, the rejected, and the broken because He himself trod that path before us.

I once anointed a woman dying of cancer, in such pain that her entire body was trembling. She had been sick for quite some time. Not many days later I received a call early in the morning from the police. Someone had been found dead and the family wanted the body blessed. I recognized

> **Every great loss demands that we choose life again.**
>
> — Rachel Remen

the address as that person's home and when I arrived the police took me aside before I went in to tell me that the woman had taken her own life. The pain had become too much. I spent a good while with the grieving husband. He was a person of sincere faith. Some months later, after he had recovered somewhat from his grief, I invited him to work with us on a team of four people being trained to visit the seriously ill and pray with them, to share their struggles. His faith and experience made of him a splendid minister of mercy and compassion. He had suffered at the foot of his wife's cross and knew well the only answer to human pain is faith in God and the cross of Jesus. Rachel Remen comments: "Every great loss demands that we choose life again. We need to grieve in order to do this. The pain we have not grieved over will always stand between us and life. When we don't grieve, a part of us becomes caught in the past like Lot's wife who, because she looked back, was turned into a pillar of salt."[17]

Sometimes I wonder if all this sounds too trite, too pious, slides too easily off the tongue. On the other hand, only last fall I pruned our rose bushes and put some horse manure around them and they are more beautiful than ever.

I was a seed of wheat. You were the sower. You buried me in the deep, dark furrow one day so long ago. I died a thousand deaths within that earth so dark, so rich, so warm, so cold, and yet I lived.

Twice I believed that it was time to bring forth fruit. But twice the storms of hatred, of scorn, froze the furrow and the earth.

Then, when it seemed to me I died my thousandth death, the rain, the sun came. And beneath its warm rays I brought forth my seeds and laid them in your hands to die again and multiply. Amen.[18]

A lovely little Hispanic second-grade girl was analyzed as having leukemia. It was devastating news to her classmates and particularly to her parents. With their young daughter in Children's Hospital of Los Angeles failing badly each day, the parents began to research what this illness was all about and work with the doctors to beat it. The young girl grew ever more frail and suffered considerable pain. The loving parents practically lived in the hospital. Every moment they could steal from work or the care of their other two daughters they spent with her, loving her. They were told the only hope lay in a bone marrow transplant that would replace the immature white blood cells with healthy ones and rid her system of the cancer.

The parents began going to local churches begging for potential donors. They discovered that the Hispanic population was uneducated in this business of bone marrow transplant. Coming from a poorer society where medical techniques are not so sophisticated, they had come to feel there was no remedy, no hope for anyone falling prey to this illness. In desperation the mother wrote to a famous Mexican boxer asking that he come and visit them, with the hope that touched by the plight of her daughter, in future meetings with the public he'd be able to help educate people, make them aware of this possible remedy for leukemia. The mother wrote, "My daughter has earned her Golden Gloves, she has fought bravely and deserves your support. Please come." One day, unannounced, the powerful boxer arrived, shy and awkward — as so often we find ourselves — not knowing what to say to a young child facing death. Only when the little girl raised her dukes in a joking way to punch him did his shyness disappear and he shared with the family a joyful visit.

During her long hospital stay, the little girl noticed that she was receiving much more love and visiting time from her parents than the other children. The parents of the other patients seemed to have found it too difficult to deal with this daily tragedy and found excuses not to come so frequently. She watched in sadness as some of the children died. She decided to take it upon herself to comfort the other youngsters, to encourage their parents. When her own parents were depressed she would always respond by saying, "Mummy, the Lord is here with us. Don't worry." In her tender age and weary body she had become a mighty dispenser of hope.

At length a donor was found and the difficult transfusion of bone marrow was accomplished. After much pain and struggle, she at length has overcome this illness, although her body will probably always show the wear and tear of the bloody battle she underwent. Last June she graduated from the eighth grade and her classmates awarded her a medal of honor, with words of thanks for her joyful courage. Hope is more than wishful thinking; hope is the power of God alive in us, moving us along to greater faith and love, to an awareness that for love nothing is impossible.

How is it that we can find God in suffering? Engraved on a plaque in the Stanford University chapel is the sentence: "It is by suffering that God has most nearly approached to man, it is by suffering that man draws most closely to God." In our suffering we can reflect on the reality that Jesus, in His humanity and in

His love for us, experienced even more anguish than we ever deal with — His physical pain, but also the sense of rejection, of abandonment by His friends, the mocking He endured. As painful as what we experience at the moment, we can say, "Lord, you understand the agony I am experiencing. Give me the faith to understand that you share it with me, that we are yoked together in carrying this heavy burden. Give me also the hope that, with you present in my heart, somehow good may come from all this. Let me share this struggle as a prayer with you for the redemption of my sisters and brothers." With this prayer in my mind and heart I can experience a sense of healing, even of hope, a sense of companionship with God. Carson McCullers crafted a beautiful statement: "The mind is like a richly woven tapestry in which the colors are distilled from the experiences of the senses, and the design drawn from the convolutions of the intellect."[19] The mind endowed with a faith that is being severely stretched can discern in all this anguish the presence of a compassionate God who is never out to punish us, but embrace and strengthen us.

The painful death of Jesus on the cross is not some cruel punishment on the part of the Father, rather it is God, incarnate in Jesus, showing us the incredible depth of His love for us. Nothing can make us more aware of the depths of God's love for us than humbly kneeling before the crucified Jesus. The greater the sacrifice, the greater the love. Never has love been given so fully and freely as on that hot Friday afternoon. Only love would venture such a maddening sacrifice.

The book of Lamentations reminds us: "The steadfast love of the LORD never ceases, his mercies never come to an end; they are new every morning, great is thy faithfulness. 'The LORD is my portion,' says my soul, 'therefore I will hope in him'" (Lam 3:22-24). The struggles we endure in life may look and smell like horse manure, but within them is the transforming power of hope and growth. That hope is not just our self-determination to make the best of a bad situation. Hope is the power of our hidden God at work within us that "is able to do far more abundantly than all we ask or think" (Eph 3:20).

QUESTIONS FOR REFLECTION:

1. What are some of the crucial moments of anguish and sorrow in my life? What have I learned from them? How did God help me through this pain and bring me healing?

2. What anger do I still bear in my soul that needs healing? Can I bring it to the Lord and let Him touch me and heal me?

3. Can I be humble enough in my moments of prayer to let Jesus wash my feet and heal me with His love? Am I humble enough to let Jesus minister to me?

4. What can I learn from Mary who endured so much at the birth and death of her son?

CHAPTER 7

Forgiveness

~~⌐

Don Santos was a joy to be around, a big tall fellow with a hearty laugh and a bad limp caused when he fell off a truck working at the local dairy. He and his wife Maria had five young boys, all active at Santo Domingo chapel in *colonia* Benito Juarez. During Mass one Sunday two of his boys were altar servers while Miguel and Eduardo sang in the youth choir. Afterwards Miguel and a few others went to visit the sick and the elderly of the *colonia*, serenading them with songs and guitars while Don Santos brought them Communion.

Early that evening young Miguel went off to his job as night watchman at a lumberyard. He was found the next morning hanging by a rope from a rafter, the victim of a break-in robbery. When the police brought Don Santos to the scene of the crime to identify his son, they told him they would do everything possible to capture and punish the guilty. Don Santos replied, "There'll be enough suffering as it is. Let them go."

Not many of us could have taken that attitude. I doubt seriously that I could have. It was the heroic voice of Jesus from the cross: "Father, forgive them; for they know not what they do" (Lk 23:34). Forgiveness does not come easily to our lips or hearts. Revenge makes its nest there and is very difficult to remove. But revenge only destroys life, eats our hearts out. Hatred poisons us. When, however, we try to get rid of these hateful feelings we find ourselves impotent. Our mind tells us it is time to let go, to be freed of that burden, yet somehow we can't seem to pry the memory, the hurt out of our heart. One viable remedy, though, is to pray to be healed. This bitterness is rooted so deeply in us that we need major spiritual heart surgery; we need God to grant us his healing, to call us forth from this tomb as he did the dead Lazarus. For, indeed, we are dead. We are unable to move ahead with life until this burden is lifted.

Healing, forgiveness, or even asking forgiveness, is sometimes a long, slow process. An example. How many parents have shared their sorrow, frustration — and sometimes anger — that their children, raised in the best Catholic schools, no longer go to Church, or are married outside of the Church, or have gotten into some type of addictive behavior. I have found it helpful to remind them of the "good thief" on the cross next to Jesus. Undoubtedly, his good Jewish mother must have spent many an hour praying that God put him back on the right path. Here he is now, on a hot Friday afternoon, nailed to a cross along with two other men. He notices that the man on the middle cross is the one getting all the attention, the booing crowd, the jeering soldiers, the mocking religious berating Him, taunting Him with the titles of "King" and "Messiah." But something about this fellow in the middle, so weak now and so bloodied by

> **Forgiveness is like plowing the soil over: new soil, fertile, ready for new seed is brought forth.**

the scourging, moves the thief to compassion, and he defends Jesus to the other thief saying, "This man has done nothing wrong" (Lk 23:41). Faith floods his heart. Those many years of the stored-up power of his mother's prayers finally break through like a dam that can no longer hold the mounting water back, and he turns to the man in the middle and says, "Jesus, remember me when you come into your kingly power" (Lk 23:42). Interesting! No one in the Bible had ever called Jesus "Jesus" before. He was always hailed as Rabbi, Teacher, Rabboni, or Master; but no one had ever addressed Him simply as "Jesus." It was as though in these few dreadful hours on the cross a bond of friendship and mutual understanding had formed between them. Both of their bodies were sagging by now, and the body fluids filling their lungs. By now both would have had difficulty in speaking. But Jesus pushes the words out, "Today you will be with me in Paradise" (Lk 23:43). Could the thief's mother have heard these final words, realized that her prayers were answered at the very last minute of her son's life? Is it possible that she was near Mary, sharing broken hearts with her as they watched together the final agony of their sons? Was she among the women the Bible refers to as standing at the foot of the cross? Whoever she was, she could tell us much about the forgiveness of God. She could teach us much about never giving up hope.

Fr. Raymond Brown, in *The Death of the Messiah*, comments on Jesus' forgiveness of the "good thief":

> The first words that the Lucan Jesus spoke to the people were in the synagogue at Nazareth, as he proclaimed release to the captives and liberty to those who were oppressed (Lk 4:18); it is only fitting that his last words addressed to another human being should fulfill that promise by offering paradise to a wrongdoer hanged on a cross.[20.]

Forgiveness is like plowing the soil over: new soil, fertile, ready for new seed is brought forth. Jesus loves us in our sinfulness, St. John reminds us, precisely because He can see that no matter how serious are the defects that scar us, the potential for growth is there; for none other than He is the creator, the gardener of our lives. "Yet with a contrite heart and a humble spirit may we be accepted" (Dan 3: Prayer of Azariah, 16), prays the prophet Daniel, precisely because it is humble, of the earth, open to new harvests. When Simon Peter was invited to follow the Lord, he shot back, "I am a sinful man, O Lord" (Lk 5:8), possibly thinking this would disqualify him from the race ahead. But Jesus saw that beneath this blustery fisherman was solid rock.

When Peter does betray the Lord, however, by denying Him three times, Jesus teaches us a great lesson on how to pardon, heal, and nourish new growth. In the last chapter of John's

Gospel, Jesus appears to the Apostles after the resurrection. The appearance is at the seaside, as was His first encounter with them, the time He had called them to follow and be "fishers of men" (Mt 4:9, Mk 1:17). In their bewilderment, the bedraggled Apostles have gone back to their old profession of fishing. Seeing that again they have spent the night without catching anything, Jesus bids them cast their nets to starboard. Suddenly John has a moment of awareness and whispers to Peter, "It is the Lord!" (Jn 21:7). With trepidation and awkwardness they move ashore and sit around the fire as Jesus fries up some of the fish for them. Peter must have squirmed as he recalled that it was but a few nights earlier that the soldiers, in the damp cold of early morning, had built a fire to warm themselves, and there he had betrayed his beloved Jesus. Now, over the hot coals Jesus looks at him again with the same eyes that looked at him across the fire at the third betrayal when the cock crowed and slips the zinger to Peter, "Do you love me?" (Jn 21:15). No dressing down, no effort to make Peter squirm, get down on his knees, and plead for mercy. Just simply put, "Do you love me?" Three times. In gentle stages the wound was healed, faith restored, friendship renewed.

As we see in the following passage from Maximus the Confessor, more is required of us than forgiveness. True love requires that we go beyond that and do good to the other, just as Jesus, knowing that Judas had already betrayed Him, does not hold back from bathing his feet at the last supper.

> The one who does not envy or is not angry, or who does not bear grudges against the one who has offended him, does not yet have love for him. For it can be that even one who does not yet love does not return evil for evil because of the commandment but in no way does he render good for evil spontaneously. Indeed, deliberately to do good to those who hate you is a mark of perfect spiritual love alone.[21]

It has become very popular these days to read that the capture of a murderer, the sentencing of someone to death, has now justly "brought closure" to the offended parties. I've never been offended that way, and have no authority to judge. But I have often wondered if that "closure" really does bring healing to the offended party, or conversion to the one who perpetrated the wrong. I've had little experience in prison ministry, but I wonder if punishment alone is the solution. Wouldn't it be to our good as well as to the prisoner to help him become more human? Wouldn't it be more healing for the victim's family to be freed of any vengeance and entrust the case to the Lord. I've read a book by a man on death row at San Quentin who, through the help of a minister, discovered the gift of contemplative prayer, and early before dawn, before the hatred of other prisoners and guards torment him, he spends an hour in quiet meditation. I have watched a videotape of Fr. Keating leading prisoners at Folsom prison in centering prayer. There was something humanizing as well as profoundly spiritual in this quiet union with a forgiving and healing God. Wouldn't they be better people and more enabled to contribute to the upbuilding of society when they left prison? Jesus has much to teach us by His healing style of forgiveness. Some theologians believe that ultimately the merciful God will gather all into His kingdom. In *Crossing the Threshold of Hope*, Pope John Paul II wrote that, although there is undoubtedly a hell, the Church has never definitively said who, if anyone, is in hell.

About ten years, ago seven-year-old Nicholas Green became the victim of a bungled highway robbery. He was traveling with his parents and little sister Eleanor from California on vacation in southern Italy. Robbers attacked and shot Nicholas while he was sleeping in the back seat of his family's car. The bullet lodged in his brain. Two days later Nicolas was dead. What happened next made worldwide news. Nicholas' parents, Reg and Maggie, decided to donate Nicholas' organs for transplant. Nicholas' heart, corneas, kidneys, pancreas cells, and liver transformed the lives of seven Italians. Nicholas' gift has transformed literally thousands of lives in Italy alone. Organ donation rates there have more than doubled. Since Nicholas' death, Reg and Maggie have become parents again, to twins, Martin and Laura. Such a life-giving, positive response to violence enables us to see Christ gloriously transfigured in these beautiful parents. Forgiving and being forgiven are privileged and powerful encounters with the Lord.

And those five sons of Don Santos? One of the four remaining is now stationed in Tijuana, a priest of the congregation founded by Mother Teresa. Could it be that the example of a forgiving father led this young man to follow Jesus, so that through this priest God would continue ministering forgiveness to those possessing hearts contrite and humble?

QUESTIONS FOR REFLECTION:

1. Who is it of whom I presently need to ask forgiveness? Who is it I need to forgive?

2. What are the feelings I experience when I have been forgiven or treated with mercy? Do I experience the compassion of Jesus in this forgiveness?

3. What emotions might Jesus have had when He washed the feet of Judas, knowing that he had already betrayed Him?

4. Jesus said to St. Catherine of Siena: "My mercy is incomparably greater than all the sins anyone could commit." Would I be able to even conceive of the possibility that ultimately all could make it to heaven, even such people as Hitler or Stalin or other mass murderers?

CHAPTER 8

Awareness

The young boy's name is easy for me to recall. He bore the same name as the founder of our Dominican Religious Order — Domingo Guzman. Domingo was 14, a Tzeltal Indian who was accompanying Fr. Louie and myself on our trek from Ocosingo to his village of La Laguna, some six miles through the Mexican Chiapas forest just north of Guatemala. Unaccustomed to riding horseback, my aching legs forced me to dismount after about two miles and lead my horse on foot the remainder of the way alongside the two of them. Several times Domingo would suddenly stop us and excitedly point out a deer or a hawk that we had not even noticed. We sophisticated men from the big city hadn't the refined skill of this young boy to notice the life and beauty hidden in the nature about us. His eyes were trained, as those who live close to the land, to see with the eyes what may not have been heard by the ears. He had developed a keen sense of awareness. He was a natural contemplative, aware of unseen deeper realities.

The native Indians, whether it be in the Andes of Peru, the mountains of Chiapas, or the bush country of Alaska are a contemplative people. You will hear it expressed in the pure music of the native flute or the rhythmic beat of the drum. They are aware of a deeper level of life. Living things form one family — the human, the animal, and God Himself. All share one world.

The Eskimo has a beautiful relationship with the animal family. He believes there exists among us a mutual respect and a mutual assistance. When the Eskimo hunter in his tiny boat snares a whale, everyone in the village comes to help capture and land it. They all pitch in to cut it up. Then, before all else they take a portion to the elderly of the village. This is in contrast to the white hunter who kills just for the excitement of the kill and often leaves the animal carcass rotting and wasted. The Eskimo and the Indian develop this respect for the environment, the animal world, and their creator through a process of growing awareness, through the teaching of their elders, and through their own life experiences of the sacredness of God's creation and its inherent balance. The elderly, having survived many winters, are respected for their age, wisdom, and skills. The Eskimo believes the whale, caribou, or seal is offering its life to nourish the people, and so out of respect and gratefulness he kills only the animals he needs for subsistence.

Awareness is the heart of contemplation. Quietly we sit at the foot of God's world and train our eyes to catch the movement of our humble God, discreetly hidden. We are like Elijah in the cave waiting for God to manifest Himself. Elijah had trained the ear of his heart to discern that presence. God was not manifest in the thunder or the mighty storm. But he caught the whisper of God's presence that wafted in on a gentle breeze. The honing of the skills of awareness, for the Christian, finds its primary tool in the workings of the Holy Spirit. It is God who forms us to the extent in which we are supple and pliable to the Spirit's movement. It is this emptying of ourselves that John of the Cross calls the "night of the senses." Quiet awareness in prayer is a discipline. Once the heart is simple and supple, the Spirit emerges gently forth from our inmost soul, praying within us. As St. John says: "Contemplation is nothing else than a secret and peaceful and loving inflow of God, which, if not hampered, fires the soul in the spirit of love."[22]

I have come to appreciate the quiet, simple ways of praying. Numerous books speak beautifully of the "how-to" of centering prayer, that quiet sitting before the Lord. In our prayer we might imagine ourselves sitting with the poor Lazarus outside the door of the rich man, waiting for a handout (see Lk 16:19-31). I try and come to prayer with love and a dedicated heart. Yet I know, being weak, my attention will not stand long at the gate, but wander the streets of my mind and nibble at those morsels that preoccupation and memory serve up. But I try to still my heart. "Be still, and know that I am God" (Ps 46:10), we are advised in the Psalms. Occasionally the heart is more tranquil. I always wait for the possible chance that the Lord will open my heart and offer me a few leftovers, a gentle whisper of love. This type of quiet prayer is not so much seeking an absence, but a presence; its goal is not so much an absence of thought but an awareness of God's presence in the soul. It is a wordless embracing of God in the heart rather than the forming of concepts in the mind. An often-quoted phrase of St. John of the Cross is "Pure contemplation consists of receiving." As Gerald May points out, however, this is not just a passive reception: "The Spanish is '*Contemplación pura consiste en recibir.*' The meaning of *recibir*, however, is not a completely passive receptivity, but rather a receiving as one might receive a guest into one's house."[23]

In the lovely church of Santo Domingo, nestled among the colonial buildings of the city of San Cristobal de las Casas, Chiapas, I have observed the native Indians come in, tilt their lit candles, let a few drops of melted wax fall onto the tile floor, and then fasten their candle to the floor. They then remain squatted in prayer until that candle, sometimes hours later, burns itself out. I have no idea how they prayed, but like Buddhist monks they remained there motionless and wordless. Psalm 131 captures it well: "I do not occupy myself with things too great and too marvelous for me. But I have calmed and quieted my soul, like a child quieted at its mother's breast" (Ps 131:2). Such is the accomplishment of a person who has achieved the virtue of purity of heart. The result is a humbleness, simplicity, and resting in the Lord.

As gentle and peaceful as the scene manifests itself, the reality is that it takes the person of prayer long and faithful years of being ground down, and crushed on more than one occasion, to reach the point where he can now truly begin to grow, to quietly surrender himself to God. Just so, the bread and wine that are changed into the Body and Blood of Christ, likewise, have been crushed and ground before they are ready for that moment of transformation. In order to take by storm St. Teresa's Interior Castle we must undertake that challenging task of emptying ourselves, following Christ's example of not clinging even to His glory with the Father. At the moment of utter powerlessness God joins us in our suffering and transforms it into our redemption for others and ourselves.

When we hunger for a life of prayer we think it may take a year or so before we are proficient in the art. However, because it seems to escape our grasp we may lose enthusiasm, feel we are not cut out for it, and immerse ourselves in activity or ministry where we can more readily measure our success. But as Thomas Merton says, the real journey of life is the journey inwards. The person beginning the journey is not the one who finally arrives. We will experience a series of crises, difficulties, or disappointments that, if open to God's grace, engender a conversion process. Our place of arrival is, as a Carthusian monk calls it, "the hermitage of our heart."[24] There we live in the life of God. "For you have died, and your life is hid with Christ in God" (Col 3:3).

> **The real journey of life is the journey inwards.**
>
> — Thomas Merton

There are those moments when in our prayer God seems so close to us, as though we could chat with Him over a cup of coffee. A sudden gift, a sudden awareness that God has somehow lightly touched us fills us with joy. But later, when we try to recapture the experience, repeat the steps in prayer that had led to this encounter, we find no way of reliving that moment. The evanescent moment of rapture evaporates as a wisp of fog vanishes gently from the hills. Our anonymous Carthusian monk puts it nicely: "You would be more than willing to forsake the earth and its joys if God allowed His glory to filter through, or deliciously fingered the keyboard of your soul." But he goes on to admit that even if that should happen it would be only fleeting. Meister Eckhart warns us that we can no more capture God in a particular method than we can capture a cow and tie it under our bench. In the long run, prayer is pure gift. As much as we strive we must realize prayer is God at work in us and it will blossom when and how He chooses. In the end, it is neither you nor I who leads the dance, it is God; you and I do not need to know the way in advance, we only need to entrust ourselves to the love of Christ, to the action of His Spirit. And so, in this struggle for relationship with God, we experience what poverty is — we experience the powerlessness and helplessness of the materially and spiritually poor. When we reach this point we can recall Eckhart's advice: "Now God wishes nothing more from you than that you get out of His way and let Him be God in you." That is hard for us because we like to be in control, we like to think we can accomplish that union if only we force ourselves harder. It is only in finally letting go and saying with Mary, "Let it be to me according to your word" (Lk 1:38), that God finally has a free hand to converse with us when and how He wills. Susan Muto adds: "When we feel most forgotten and forsaken, like Jesus in Gethsemane, at that moment of supreme agony by human standards, we may be most intimately united with God. He leads us through this narrow way of the cross so that we can pass from death to self to new life in Him."[25]

Recently, I was perched on a rock overlooking the sea watching in amusement a cute sea otter floating on its back, his arms crossed placidly on its chest, gently rising and falling with the movement of the waves. How I wish my prayer could be like that, resting in the Lord, letting Him support me. At times, though, I find myself flummoxed, like a fish tangled in a net of distractions and worries.

Just sit quietly as though you were on a bench overlooking the ocean, quietly drinking in the beauty of the scene. Be aware that God is in your deepest heart. He does not need to be entertained with brilliant thoughts or beautiful insights. God simply longs to share your heart. If you notice that your mind is galloping like a runaway horse, just quietly focus on your breathing, or repeat a simple word, like "Lord" or "peace," and ease back to centeredness. What God sees is your intention to be with Him. Prayer looks out all the time toward God and stretches toward Him with desire. Jeremy Taylor describes it wonderfully when he says: "Prayer is only the body of the bird. Desires are its wings!" And then we can only wait for God's movement, like the angel that touches the water at Bethsaida, or the gentle breeze that spoke to Elijah. At that moment we realize it is not we who are the ones praying, but that the Spirit of God is the one praying from within us.

Like the person who comes to appreciate poetry or classical music, or like young Domingo, we learn how to listen and how to see what is beyond the surface. Maybe at some point in our contemplative lives we might be enabled to understand what Eckhart says, "The eye by which I see God is the same one by which He sees me."

We are terrified of silence. If we are meeting a person for the first time, we dread those moments when suddenly the conversation skids to a stop and we don't know how to pick it up again. I have filed away mental notes of what to say should an ebullient conversation suddenly run out of gas. Modern technology is that great enabler of the quick escape. Cell phones have multiplied like rabbits, facilitating a quick dodge from silence to an inane chit-chat with someone, anyone, on the other end. We have our teeth drilled while being distracted by a divertimento of Mozart, our nerves jangled at an intersection waiting for a red light to change as our car begins to sway in sync with the decibels of hard metal rock crashing upon us in waves from the car revved up next to us. We insulate ourselves with noise, building an iron curtain to keep at bay any possibility of the sounds of silence.

We are afraid of silence because we might then actually have to think; we may have to look inward, and we are afraid that we will discover there is no "there" there. Thomas Merton writes that we are afraid to look inward, fearing we will only find a giant vacuum. And so, fearful that we might be sucked into this black hole, we scramble out by any distraction we can get our hands on — busyness, noise, the violence of TV and movies, computer pornography that would have made Salome blush. Rather rapidly, though, our society becomes sated and we have to ratchet up to another level the volume and blatant quality of our diversions. Like drugs, we become immune to them, and have to boost the dose another notch higher to keep our attention riveted and escape looking inward. We end up making gods of all these escapes rather than finding the true God in the silence of our hearts. The person of prayer has learned that if we look inward and get beyond the first awkward steps of silence we discover the immense richness of God.

Recently I made a quiet retreat at a Camoldolese monastery set tranquilly on a piece of the rugged California coast overlooking the sea. Several nights I went outside to spend time in prayer under the stars. Sitting there quietly in the pure darkness I discovered a world I had long forgotten. There on this mountaintop with no glaring city lights to compete with nature I rediscovered a myriad of stars that shone out in sparkling splendor. With no distracting light to diffuse their brilliance, they shimmered in gospel clarity. So it is with silence. When we clear the air of noisy distractions we may in some distinct way hear the quiet whisper of God's voice.

In our busy world, where time is the greatest treasure we have, it is difficult for us to dedicate time — or "waste time" as some might say — to simply be with our family, our loved ones, our God. Like those tempting sirens that sang lustily to woo mighty Odysseus and his men and waylay them from ever making it home, the demands on our time are hard to resist. But only in prayerful intimacy with God, loving presence with family and friends, will we discover a sense of unity, meaning, and joy in our lives.

Prayer, quiet union with God, is not an escape. It is not a seeking for a God who can fill my needs because no one else seems to appreciate me or gives a darn about me. Our life of prayer is not an escape from a hostile world, a world in which we may have felt hurt, or which is fomenting my tilt toward paranoia. It is more than a talking *to* God; it is an awareness of the indwelling of God who prays with us, and within us in the Spirit. Our life of prayer is a rootedness in God that allows us to love others as God loves us. Our life with God moves us from a self-centeredness to a Christ-centeredness, and finally to a cosmic Christ-centeredness, finding Christ at the core still point of the universe and all its inhabitants. A life of prayer that is an escape from the people we feel don't appreciate us, a pouting mood of playing the martyr, is not a healthy life of prayer. Anthony de Mello says "When you desire holiness for yourself you feed the very greed and ambition that make you so selfish and vain and unholy."[26]

Contemplative silence also allows us to find other ways in which God makes himself present to us. Like a familiar face that emerges from the crowd, like a deer in the forest that you suddenly notice noticing you, silence nurtures a gentle awareness, a gentle emergence of consciousness that may allow us to discern how God has guided us in life, been with us at times we had not noticed before; it grants me the gift of suddenly realizing that it is no longer "I who live, but Christ who lives in me" (Gal 2:20), that Christ is my life. Being silently with the Lord is also a healing experience. Who hasn't felt joy and healing when in the life-giving presence of a beloved friend? The same is true of being present to the Lord, although that is not our primary purpose for going to Him in prayer. "Some people love

God the way they love their cow: for its milk and cheese," warns our medieval mystic Eckhart.

Or, as Thomas Merton cautions us: "The important thing in contemplation is not gratification and rest, but awareness, life, creativity, and freedom." A side effect, however, of being with God is a sense of joy, peace, a deeper sense of self, a deep interior healing of all those bruises, and a rinsing out of the garbage that we have gathered in our journey through life.

Prayers of praise and petition, reading of spiritual books and meditation on favorite psalms and passages from the Bible are the varied colors and textures that weave together a friendship and trust between the person and our God. But just as the indwelling Spirit, with our cooperation, accomplishes all these, so too moments of silent prayer, of thoughtless thought are open to us. However, they are mercurial and beyond our grasp. Like the boat with its sails unfurled, we can only open our soul and hope for the breeze of the Spirit to blow. John of the Cross says, "The soul delights in finding itself alone with God and in gazing on Him with love, without any particular consideration."[27] This communion simplifies and purifies the soul; it is the experience of personhood.

The contemplative's skill of seeing the deeper reality of life and God's subtle presence in our lives is what often calls this person to be a prophet, a person concerned for justice. "For the kingdom of God does not mean food and drink but righteousness and peace and joy in the Holy Spirit" (Rom 14:17). Persons of prayer, or of contemplative soul, or those who have suffered greatly, somehow develop a more penetrating awareness of God's presence in His handiwork, the human person. So it is people like Abraham Lincoln, Mohatma Ghandi, Dorothy Day, St. Catherine of Siena, Oscar Romero, and Thomas Merton who from their storehouse of wisdom speak forth against the injustices inflicted upon the downtrodden. We have the prophets to thank for the great insight that religion is not a specialized activity of a person's life, but a quality and attitude in all his activities, a total way of being governed by the orientation of his spirit toward God, a contemplative awareness of God's imminent presence in all of creation.

God speaks to us not only in silent, gentle movements of our soul, but also in gentle movements of events. Ray Hudson has written a fine book on the Aleut culture of southwestern Alaska, which he has entitled *Moments Rightly Placed*.[28] It is a rich expression that I would like to apply to what we so often call "luck." "Wasn't it lucky I found that job?" Or "Wasn't it lucky I bumped into you today?" I believe it can well be more than just "luck," but the gentle way of God bringing a time of new growth into our lives. Let me share such a moment with you, one that may help you in seeing a "lucky" or even an "unlucky" episode in your life from a different, sharper perspective.

Jim and I had been high school buddies. After his service in the Navy, he married and went to a university near the seminary where I was studying. He and his wife would come by every "visiting Sunday" — in days when seminarians were considerably more restricted than at present — bringing along a much-appreciated chocolate milkshake. Jim and his wife became like brother and sister, companions offering the warmth of friendship.

However, after finishing our studies, we lost track of each other. A good number of years later I was in Washington, D.C., for a meeting and took advantage of a free moment to explore the museums and historic buildings. Having ascended the Washington Monument and taken in the view, I returned to the elevator. As I walked into the crowded elevator car, there directly in front of me were Jim and his wife and their young boys. It was a startling encounter, a blessed event that allowed us to renew and deepen a friendship that proved to be life-long and very important for both of us. He and I helped each other through some difficult times, he in his marriage, and me in my own vocation. In our later years we were able to spend a good bit of free time together, and I was blessed by being around in his final illness and comforting him — a very religious person — when on his deathbed he experienced not only great pain but also deep anxiety. After the funeral, his wife was able to say that the best gift I ever gave him was a sense of peace and consolation in his final moments. That chance meeting at the top of the Washington Monument was indeed more than "luck," it was "a moment rightly placed," rightly and carefully placed by God, a special gift to him, his family, and myself.

Whenever someone goes off on a trip or adventure, I no longer say, "Good luck," but rather, "Go with God" — *Vaya con Dios.*

QUESTIONS FOR REFLECTION:

1. What encounters in my life can I see were "moments rightly chosen" by God, and not just "luck"?

2. How does deepening my prayer life allow me to see life from a different perspective and give me different values and goals?

3. How is it that I dodge and delay the journey inward?

4. In reflecting on my weaknesses and strengths, do I recognize them as occasions or resources for growing more fully in the life of the Spirit?

CHAPTER 9

Thirsting for God

Three hours outside Mexicali lie a few tiny villages on a strip of land snuggled up against the westward mountains, nourished by mountain streams and natural oases, bravely fending off the scorching desert lying eastward. Once a month a priest and a few Sisters from our parish would travel out to offer catechism and Mass to the small flock of Mexican farmers living there. Leaving the highway there is a gravel road leading to the villages. It is so rugged that by the time you arrive screws and bolts are coming loose from the van as well as inside your head. So we preferred going straight across the dry lakebed, Laguna Salada. The experience was like an extraterrestrial drive across the surface of the moon. After more than an hour of coursing over hard, barren desert sand, the Promised Land, the land of milk and honey, began to appear on the horizon. As we drew near we could make out fields of wheat, vast vineyards of grapes, and scores of date palms. Amazing what miracles a bit of water oozing from natural springs and oases can perform.

The workers irrigate the vineyard by the "Israeli method." That is, rather than irrigating by ditch or sprinkler, methods that allow for quick evaporation and loss of water, irrigation is done through plastic tubes that drip water at each vine on the plant roots through single holes drilled in the pipe. The only hazards then are the coyotes that sneak down at night to chew open the tubes and drink to their hearts' delight. A few of the old timers spend the night in vigil to shoot the coyotes and drape their bodies over the fences made of thorny Ocotillo branches that divide up the farmland.

Lunching on tacos and menudo, you cannot doubt as you look about at the landscape of mountains, desert, and wells, that you are standing on land very similar to that on which Jesus walked. Christians, Jews, and Moslems all trace their roots back to the desert, that sacred place of beauty and danger. In the awesome silence of the desert God has spoken to our ancestors, Abraham, Moses, and on down to John the Baptist. Finally, he speaks to Jesus himself. "Jesus, full of the Holy Spirit, returned from the Jordan, and was led by the Spirit for forty days in the wilderness, tempted by the devil" (Lk 4:1-3).

Desert life is geared to survival. Survival means finding water. Without it, plants, animals, and humans dehydrate and die. So many of our brothers and sisters from Mexico and Central America, longing for a chance to provide a better living for their families back home, have miserably died attempting to cross the deserts along our southwestern border. Desert areas often receive only an inch or two of rain in the entire year. Conservation of water is the sole means of surviving in these climes. Nature is amazing in its ingenuity to devise survival techniques.

> **O God, thou art my God, I seek thee, my soul thirsts for thee; my flesh faints for thee, as in a dry and weary land where no water is.**
>
> — Ps 63:1

The familiar large barrel cactus stores water in its innermost part and protects itself from the intruder by a myriad of large, very sharp needles. The bush that we Americans call the creosote plant is called by the Mexicans *la gobernadora,* "the governess," because it spreads out its roots along the surface of the soil for a good 12 feet in each direction, absorbing all the moisture it can, thereby "governing" her territory, preventing any other plant from growing in its area. The beautiful ocotillo, which grows up to twenty or more feet in height, is covered with thorns under which are tiny leaves about the size of your thumbnail. When they sense rain coming, the leaves gradually come out to catch the water, and when the heat returns the leaves withdraw under the thorns so that the water in them is not dried by the sun's rays.

The desert was home for the Hebrew people and so water was an essential element of life for them. Consequently, when Jesus, in the crush of a large religious festival, gets up and shouts out that He is the source of living water, people must have stopped short and listened attentively.

> On the last day of the feast, the great day, Jesus stood up and proclaimed, "If any one thirst, let him come to me and drink. He who believes in me, as the scripture has said, 'Out of his heart shall flow rivers of living water'" (Jn 7:37-38).

Jesus' statement takes on power and significance by the fact that He "cried out" during the festivities of the Feast of Tabernacles, a feast second in importance only to the Jewish feast of Pentecost. It took place in the autumn of the year at harvest time. Throughout this period of harvesting grapes and other fruits, the farmers and their families would have camped outdoors in huts, possibly the reason it came to be called also the "Feast of Booths." In any case, it was an agricultural feast that could have been instituted only after Israel had settled down to farm life in Canaan. It was a time of joy, feasting, and dancing; a time when psalms of praise were sung and liturgical functions performed throughout eight days of celebration. Because of its importance in the lives of the people, Solomon centuries earlier had chosen this occasion on which to dedicate the magnificent temple in Jerusalem, a fact that in turn heightened the importance of the feast and added a new meaning to it.

It is only natural that, being an agricultural feast, water was of supreme significance and consequently played a major role in the symbols used during the liturgical rites. On each day of the octave, water was drawn with great solemnity from the Pool of Siloam and brought in golden vessels to the temple, where it was poured out in the southwest corner of the altar of holocausts.

And so it was in this context that Jesus "stood up and proclaimed, 'if any one thirst, let him come to me and drink'" (Jn 7:37). This humble Jesus of Nazareth insinuates that He is the new temple from which living waters flow, replacing the temple in Jerusalem as the font of life and worship.

We find in the Gospel of John seven important water episodes. We all are aware that for the Jewish people the number seven signifies fullness, completeness. The seven events are:

1. Jesus' first miracle, at the wedding feast at Cana, when He changes water into wine (Jn 2:1-11).
2. Jesus' conversation with Nicodemus, when He speaks about rebirth through baptism by water (Jn 3:1-8).
3. Jesus' meeting with the Samaritan woman at the well (Jn 4:7-30).
4. Jesus' healing of the man at the pool of Bethzatha (Jn 5:2-9).
5. Jesus identifying himself as the source of living waters (Jn 7:37-38).
6. Jesus healing the man born blind after telling him to wash in the pool of Siloam (Jn 9:1-2).
7. The water that flows from the side of Christ when He is pierced by a spear while on the cross (Jn 19:34).

The seventh, of course, is the culmination, for in the very moment of His death Jesus gives life. The blood and water that flow from His side signify the power of life transmitted to us in the sacraments of baptism and the Eucharist.[29]

We, too, thirst for life. We stretch out our roots in search of someone who will fill that life with love, with meaning and joy, with understanding and acceptance. Hopefully we will one day realize that person is Jesus, our beloved friend who delights in playing hide and seek with us. It may take us a long time to find Him, or better, to let Him find us. Or as Catherine LaCugna puts it: "One finds God because one is already found by God. Anything we would find on our own would not be GOD." We may search for other ways to satisfy our hunger and thirst, but in the long run, as Augustine puts it: "Our hearts are restless until they rest in you."

Experts who analyze this human thirst, who analyze our worries tell us that chief among them is our need for companionship, our dread of being alone. Loneliness is a fear provoking experience. By God's will and design we are not born to be alone. We search for family, friends, and sometimes compassionate strangers to share moments, joyful or sorrowful, that call for human companionship. At no time on the journey is this need more deeply felt than when we grow weak with the passing of time, and when the way, winding and uphill, narrows to the point that the road and time itself come to an end.

Memory is very important for our spiritual growth. It is essential to etch on our memory those times in life when we experienced the presence of Jesus, His peace, His healing, and His strength. The moment of first encounter with Jesus was so engraved in the memory of John the Apostle that he remembers even the hour they first met: "It was about the tenth hour" (Jn 1:39), which was four in the afternoon. We might recall the first time in our youth we sensed a real belief in Him, or later when we experienced His help in a difficult situation. It is like building a fence. Each of our experiences of Jesus is like another post extending further this marvelous friendship. We chart this faithful friendship from post to post, event to event. When a moment of doubt strikes us, or an occasion of fear, we then must look back and see that long stretch of fence and know that Jesus who has ever been with us will not abandon us now. That lifelong friendship will lead us especially through the time of death to the newness of life. St. Gregory of Nazianzus writes that a person "will not grow old in spirit, but will accept dissolution as the moment fixed for the freedom which must come. Gently he will cross into the beyond, where there is neither youth, nor old age, but where all are perfect in spiritual maturity."[30] If with God's grace we've been able to build a hermitage in our heart, we might be able to own the words of the Carthusian, William of Saint-Thierry: "He with whom God is, is never less alone than when he is alone. For then he can enjoy his joy, then he is his own to enjoy God in himself and himself in God."[31]

Psalm 63, used in the Church's morning psalms on every major feast, phrases it beautifully:

> O God, thou art my God, I seek thee, my soul thirsts for thee; my flesh faints for thee, as in a dry and weary land where no water is. So I have looked upon thee in the sanctuary, beholding thy power and glory. Because thy steadfast love is better than life, my lips will praise thee (Ps 63:1-3).

I have owned those words and made them mine: "like a dry and weary land without water, I long for you, O God," as it reads in another translation.

I have seen parched, baked soil in dried up lakebeds in the desert with their patterned veins of cracks and fissures, and thought, "Yes, that is how I long for the Lord." A thirst for the goodness of the Lord so deep that I ached, a thirst to experience His presence, to praise Him for His faithfulness and patience with me when I was so busy talking and teaching about the Lord that I took so little time to talk with Him. I took such pride in accomplishments and so little time simply to be, to reflect that Mary's greatest quality was her being: "My soul magnifies the Lord" (Lk 1:46) — her very being proclaimed the greatness of the Lord.

Hopefully, sometime in your life you will have the special joy of seeing the desert in bloom. It is miraculous what a little bit of spring rain can do to transform the sandy vastness into a garden of shimmering colorful and exotic plants, from tiniest bluebonnets to mighty boojum elephant trees and the thorn-filled ocotillo bushes with their olive drab, thumbnail sized leaves and fiery red crown, symbolic of the tongue of the Spirit's fire. If we drink deeply of the Lord, we too will also be transformed into exotic, fragrant beauties in the Garden of the Lord. All for His praise and glory.

> The one who through asceticism and contemplation has known how to dig in himself the wells of virtue and knowledge as did the patriarchs will find Christ within as the spring of life. Wisdom bids us to drink from it, saying, "Drink water from your own cistern, flowing water from your own well" (Prov 5:15). If we do this we shall discover that his treasures are present within us (Maximus the Confessor).[32]

QUESTIONS FOR REFLECTION:

1. What goals and choices that I have made in my life demonstrate my longing, my thirst for God?

2. In what ways in my prayer and contemplation do I experience Christ as the spring, the source of my life?

3. The contemplative path is a way of discovering a secret hidden deep within our hearts. When I pray, do I experience the Holy Spirit as the one who is praying to God with me from the very depths of my soul?

4. What are some of those memories that weave together the history of my intimate friendship with Jesus?

CHAPTER 10

Gratefulness

How odd! Everyone here is so gracious, so grateful, always saying, "Thank you, Father," for this, or, "Thank you," for that. Yet here we were in the midst of a large leprosarium, some several thousand people, a mixture of lepers and *sanos* — healthy ones. In some cases it was the wife who was a leper and the husband not. In other families it was the opposite. Possibly both were lepers and the children not, or again, perhaps the reverse. Tala, one hour distant from Manila, was an old military barracks from World War II that had been converted into a refuge for the many Filipino lepers who came mostly from "the provinces," the more remote and poorer areas.

It was astounding to encounter such gratefulness in people one would expect would be the most miserable of all. Those who were lepers indeed had reason to be sad and overwhelmed, for the disease is very demeaning. When I accompanied the chaplain to the various compounds, he would never let me stop and attempt to console the patients, but rather would play like a jolly Santa Claus with them or use me as the butt of a joke to get them to laugh. He once chided me when I stayed too long with one patient and, pulling me away, said there wasn't anything I could say that would alleviate her sadness. "Just do something crazy or funny to get them out of themselves for a bit," he advised.

My first Sunday there, I discovered the reason for this constant "Thank you, Father." After the 9:00 A.M. Mass in the large Quonset hut that served as the church, the priest would retire to his house several blocks away. There, the ladies had set up a chair with a table behind it and were at the ready to hand him bags of candy they had prepared beforehand. The children eagerly formed into two lines, anxiously waiting their moment to get candy. However, there were two important conditions before the children could get their longed-for prize. One was that the candy was given only to lepers, not to the *sanos*, the "healthy ones." The other was that a child needed to say, "Thank you, Father," when given the gift. So if the chaplain held out his hand with the bag of goodies and there was no immediate, "Thank you, Father," he would jerk it back and the child would have to go away literally empty-handed. Forty years of doing this Sunday after Sunday drilled home a deeply rooted habit of gratefulness, an easy flowing "thank you" for any kindness shown.

The next Sunday, as the children gleefully waited for their candy, a young boy, very obviously and tragically leprous, finally worked his way to the front of the line. We were all befuddled when Father taunted him that he was not a leper and what was he doing here asking for candy. The boy, dumbfounded, stood his ground and stated that yes, indeed, he was a leper. After a few rounds of this the priest finally asked him, "Are you really a leper?" When the boy responded in the affirmative, the priest asked again, "Do you want to be a leper?" And the boy, laughing, said, "Yes — so I can have the candy," and grabbing it ran off squealing with delight.

For forty years the priest had given his life to these people, reminding them that Jesus, like the lepers of his own day, knew what it was like to be ostracized by one's own, and so Jesus was here among them to give their lives dignity and meaning. He did this through the hands of Fr. Hofstee, who built them a grammar school, high school, and even a college. Only lepers were hired to be teachers, and proudly they handed on their knowledge, faith, and experience. They had learned from this tough Dutchman that they were worthy of respect and dignity, that despite the deformity of their body, in their own special way they are God's work of art. Beauty is more than skin deep.

How often have I whined when I had a headache or was pained by arthritis? How often have I have hardened my heart at God when things went wrong? Haven't we caught ourselves grumbling and grousing because the traffic is bottled up, the neighbors rowdy, or the teenagers driving us up the wall? Haven't we sometimes suddenly been brought up short when we realized how much we had taken our parents for granted, never offered a word of thanks for the times they stayed up caring for us, worrying about us, sacrificed their time and desires that we'd have a good home, a good education? How often we have blamed God when things went wrong. How often we have begged God for favors, but how seldom we have taken time to give Him thanks.

> **In the end, gratitude is the root of all virtue. It lies at the base of love and charity.**
>
> — Ronald Rolheiser

Gratefulness is a learned virtue, an opening of our eyes to see how we've been blessed, an opening of our heart in return because God has loved us first, without any merit or effort on our part. "In the end, gratitude is the root of all virtue. It lies at the base of love and charity,"[33] notes Ronald Rolheiser. A simple way of being grateful and offering a prayer of thanksgiving is to feel your pulse for a moment. Each next heartbeat is a gift from God. We don't do anything to bring it about except joyfully receive it. Anyone with respiratory problems can tell you how frightening it is at times when you are not sure the next breath will come or not. All the beautiful joys of life are gifts — love, friendship, health, and happiness. We can't purchase them at the local supermarket. For that matter, so are the gifts of faith, hope, and love. What would we do without these? Once received, though, we must work at developing them, deepening them, or like muscles we don't often use, they will atrophy and die. Like a beautiful flower we do not keep the beauty God has given us closed in upon itself. We need to let the petals open to show the world God's beauty mirrored in us, to share our gifts and graces with others, and to let our thankfulness be reflected back to Him.

In a sense we are all lepers. Our leprosy may not be that of the body but of the spirit. Our strain of leprosy might be pride, greed, a hunger for power and control, or, conversely, simply ennui, bored with life, no sense of wonder, no spark of enthusiasm. We are the walking dead, zombies without hearts, or on the contrary zealots with our hearts in the wrong place.

In moments of honesty, we can admit we are sinful. As St. Paul confesses, even on those occasions when we attempt to do good we end up behaving in sinful, self-centered ways. We may try to look good before God and neighbor, pretend we are something we are not. Like the phantom of the opera, we cover our face with a mask, our true self with a false persona, afraid of the day the world will discover that under the mask lay the face of a leper.

At some moment in our life, though, Jesus will arrive on His white horse, as in the Apocalypse, to raise us to life and love us beyond our wildest dreams. He may possibly need to knock us off our horse first. My prayer is that I will be humble enough to let Him transform me with His wand of amazing grace.

I was jolted by such a transforming moment when I was only a month from high school graduation. I was a model student, but in a reckless moment a few other classmates and I suddenly went giddy and disrupted class. I was not just sent out of the room. I was sent home. My premature arrival home startled my mother, and when I explained the reason she angrily replied that she "disowned me." An only child, I was devastated and like a dog with his tail between his legs slunk out to the back corner of our grapefruit grove and sat and wept the rest of the day. As dusk descended, my father came out and said that I could come home now. Like Lazarus, I rose from my tomb, repentant and relieved to be restored to life.

But this had an effect on my spiritual life that my saintly mother never intended, and of which I remained ignorant until much later in life when, working with the materially poor, I discovered the richness of God's love. The effect of my mother's chastening was that henceforth I was always striving to be loved and accepted by accomplishing great deeds. A mixture of Catholic guilt and American desire for efficiency and productivity made of me a hybrid workaholic. Like an eager Boy Scout, I kept piling up merit badges of multifarious good works, striving to be the best Eagle Scout in God's troop. I was convinced that only in pleasing others, amazing others by my zeal and proficiency, could I win their love. I recall years later, when our parish staff took a day off together for prayer and planning and time for sharing a bit of our life stories with each other that I listed all the places where I had been pastor, the churches I built, and my various accomplishments. One of the associate pastors replied, "Well. Paul, that's fine, but now tell us *who* you are." That insight on his part was a great awakening and a special gift.

Gratefulness, rather, is our path to growth. We need to take to heart the words of St. Paul to the Ephesians: "But God, who is rich in mercy, out of the great love with which he loved us, even when we were dead through our trespasses, made us alive together with Christ . . . For by grace you have been saved through faith, and this is not your own doing; it is the gift of God — not because of works" (Eph 2:4, 8-9). There is no way we can ever earn His love. It is always pure gift. Fr. Richard Rohr is always reminding us that we should not have the mentality that God will love me if I change my sinful ways; but rather that because He first loved me, I am enabled to change my sinful ways. His love is often more readily available to the broken among us, the failures, the sinners, to those who are childlike, because they already know they are helpless to earn it. We who feel we have worked so hard to "earn" God's love will identify with the older brother in the parable of the prodigal son, angry that this wayfaring, lazy, prostituted sinner, who's not worth a darn, is getting the Father's love and the fatted calf. If we but understood that we are already loved, we would rather be able to rejoice at our brother's good fortune and relish in the party as well.

What I am trying to get at is that gratefulness is a greater motivator than guilt. Awareness of God's love and our response in gratitude for that love allows us to grow much more than being motivated by guilt or countless good intentions made and quickly forgotten. Growing in holiness is not the accomplishment of spiritual pushups. Growing in holiness is growing in self-forgetful love by allowing God's spirit within us the freedom to blossom forth. To repeat again what Eckhart says: "Get out of the way and let God be God within you." Or, as St. Paul put it, "I planted, Apollos watered, but God gave the growth" (1 Cor 3:6).

I do not mean to infer that virtues need not be developed, or fasting and ascetical practices entered into. They are indeed necessary; they are foundational. They are a clearing of the ground so that the plant of God's love may grow. Books on yoga encourage fasting as a way of purifying the body. The traditional teaching of the Church is that fasting is also a purifying of the spirit, an acknowledgement of our hunger for God, a form of showing our sincerity, and a pleading for God's graces. As Jesus tells us, God scatters the seed, but it is up to us to take out the rocks and spade in fertile soil so that the seed will grow. We do that by fasting, prayer, and charity. But the growth is from the plant itself. We water it with our love and Jesus nourishes it with His blood and it grows and blooms for the glory of God.

Very recently, I came back from some missionary work on a small Aleutian island. Because of stormy winter weather I could not return by seaplane but hitched a ride on a 110-foot crab fishing boat. The seas were rough, so the first item given me as I boarded was a plastic garbage bag to use for seasickness. When we hit a strait where the Bering Sea and the Pacific Ocean collide, it was like entering God's giant washing machine as we were tumbled and rolled in every direction. I then understood why the Aleutians have been called the place "where the sea breaks its back." I came to admire the Alaska fishermen, a profession that is ranked by insurance companies as the most dangerous in our country. In the winter season of fishing for crab, seas are high and water is freezing. As the waves crash over the ship there are days in which, because of freezing cold, the water quickly begins to freeze and ice builds up on the masts and superstructure of the ship. The men have to struggle on the slippery decks with baseball bats and sledgehammers to break off chunks of ice, otherwise the ice will continue to build up and the weight will cause the boat to capsize.

Such are the ways, then, in which we cooperate with God's grace to keep His life growing within us: we prepare the ground and protect the plant as it grows; we clear the decks of excess baggage so that the boat can run its true course. The first step, though, is God's: showering His love upon us. We cooperate in removing obstacles that prohibit the freedom of movement of that love. The gift of grace is the gift of God's life and action within us, which ennobles us and enables us to share His divinity. St. Irenaeus writes: "... the Word of God, Jesus Christ our Lord, who because of his immeasurable love became what we are in order to make us what he is."[34]

These long-suffering persons at Tala, whose bodies were being eaten away by leprosy like acid stripping the plating off metal, were trained to be grateful for the gift of life. They had learned that the treasured gift of life is more precious than the wrapping it comes in. God's gracious love makes of each of us something beautiful. Some of us might be roses, some lilies, and others odd-looking desert ocotillos that bloom gloriously in the spring and whose brilliant red flowers are the flaming colors of the Pentecost Spirit of God. The heavenly gardener takes great delight in His glorious garden.

> Rejoice always, pray constantly, give thanks in all circumstances; for this is the will of God in Christ Jesus for you (1 Thess 5:16-18).

⌐⊃

QUESTIONS FOR REFLECTION:

1. When I quiet myself down and feel my pulse or gently listen to my breathing, am I able to experience the immanent presence of God "who knit me together in my mother's womb" (Ps 139:13)? Do I experience a feeling of gratefulness?

2. In what ways can I build within myself a greater sense of gratitude toward God?

3. When I realize that all that I have and all that I am come from God's generosity, what begins to happen to my attitudes toward myself and others?

4. How would I explain to others the quote from Fr. Rolheiser: "In the end, gratitude is the root of all virtue"?

CHAPTER 11

Don't Judge by Appearances

~~~

It was the Saturday before Christmas, and I still had a few last minute gifts to purchase. Bundled up with several layers of sweaters, a heavy cap, and gloves I set off for the department store three blocks down 4th Avenue from the cathedral. I walked briskly along the main street of Anchorage in minus 10-degree weather. Several hundred yards from the store, I noticed ahead at the entrance to the mall an Eskimo ringing the Salvation Army bell and holding out his bucket for donations. Heavily clothed and wearing an enormous fur head covering, he was shuffling about, stomping his feet to keep warm. I admired his stamina. I hesitated at what to do, as I needed all the money I had in my pocket for my gifts. Suddenly I spotted a small side entry door just this side of the Eskimo and his bucket. I slipped into the safe harbor of Penney's and did my shopping. I was careful to exit the store by going out the 5th Avenue exit and thus avoid the Eskimo as well as shield a guilty conscience.

Later that afternoon I went over to the church to hear confessions. I had barely gotten settled when the door opened that would allow in those who wish to confess face to face. And what to my wondering eyes did appear but that same Eskimo. I cringed, hoping he wouldn't recognize me as the tightwad who snuck off into the store. He was quite large and it took him some time to unburden himself of his huge jacket and headpiece and fold them up on the floor. He sat down and said, "Father, before making my confession, I have to say that I'm really discouraged. I've been standing for several hours out in that cold and people just keep walking by without putting money in my bucket." Guilt and embarrassment welled up within me as I struggled with what to say. Suddenly I just blurted out: "Don't judge by appearances! Maybe they had already given to another Salvation Army person. Maybe they were intending to give their donation to the St. Vincent de Paul society."

Don't judge by appearances! How many times I have misjudged people. How often I have seen the speck in someone else's eye, but not the beam in my own. We live in a world that judges by appearances. We think poor people are just lazy, the elderly a burden to society, that foreigners enter our country to sponge off of us. Only later do we realize they may well have been a blessing in disguise. The Pharisee sat in the front of the temple and mocked the fellow in the back row. "God, I thank thee that I am not like other men, extortioners, unjust, adulterers, or even like this tax collector" (Lk 18:11). In his pride he got it all backward. He judged by appearances and was blind to a faith and humility in that supposed sinner that was greater than his own.

When I reflect on why I judge others I come to the sad conclusion that there is some kind of insecurity in me, something in me that says that if this individual is better than me, then I am no good. So I will criticize them and put them down to lessen that threat. But why do I have this need of estimating myself as good as or better than another? Possibly it is because of the American culture in which we live, where there is such emphasis on being number one, of being able to boast about how much I have accomplished. I have this notion that if I have been busy and done a lot, I have achieved goodness. When I first began living in Mexico, I found it interesting that when I was meeting a person for the first time and would ask a very typical American question, "Well, what do you do for a living?" I would get these blank stares, these puzzled looks, until I explained I was asking where they worked, what profession they had. I came to learn that the Mexican, the various nations of Eskimos, and many other cultures identify themselves first as a member of a family — it is the family that is most important and gives you meaning and identity — your profession is something secondary.

I also have come to realize that my tendency to put others down was that I hadn't accepted my goodness as something God-given, a gift from the creator, a love that didn't have to be purchased by proving oneself or by some type of negotiating process, some type of *quid pro quo* bargaining. I came to find that one of the benefits of centering prayer is that it helps me realize I indeed am loved, that I don't have to prove myself, that in the Lord lies my love and my security. "The LORD is my rock, and my fortress, and my deliverer, my God, my rock, in whom I take refuge" (Ps 18:2). A life of prayer roots us in Christ and it is this friendship that above all gives us identity and meaning, and moves us from a need to prove ourselves to an ability to be free, at ease, in the love of Christ. In prayer our hearts are calmed, we find a peace that takes away anxiety, fear, and insecurity. Someone once told me that, as in the parable of the lost sheep, when the young lamb is lost, like us, its heart begins to race. So when the shepherd finds the lost sheep he holds it to his gently beating heart and that calms down the frightened animal. The poor in spirit realize their great richness is the Lord's love for them, and this gives them a self-respect, a healthy awareness of their goodness, a liberty that sets them free from the need to be judgmental or negatively critical of others. This I have learned from the humble people with whom I have been blessed to share my life.

> **Faith is the gift that allows us to see beyond the surface, beyond the appearance and discover the substance beneath.**

Presiding at the liturgy with the people who work in the canneries far out in the Aleutian Islands has been one of those humbling experiences. At first blush, it would be easy to describe them as lower-level blue collar workers. Fishing ports have some pretty rough characters, and alcoholism easily leads them into destructive behavior — destructive to themselves as well as to the community. The isolation, harsh weather, and dormitory style living can be hard for some to bear and they look for diversions that easily get them into trouble. Working in the canneries twelve hours a day with only one day off in every fourteen can become weary drudgery. I was, however, humbled to discover how many have a deep desire of living a truly Christian life in the midst of a work environment that is not necessarily very conducive to a life of prayer and virtue. I heard confessions as sincere and innocent as any I have ever heard. I have made the acquaintance of Hispanic, Filipino, Vietnamese, and African Americans who work such long and tiring hours so that they can send their earnings home to support their families who live practically half a world away. One Filipino lady put it so simply: "I've been here four years now and I think maybe in four years more I will have done my best for my family, and I'll be able to go home." She held no grudge, bore no complaints that she had spent so much time in a place that offered her so few comforts while challenging her with a climate and culture so different from where she had been raised and married. Like the migrant field workers who toil so hard with little job security, these people make such sacrifices for their families that I shared with them in a Sunday homily that I could clearly see the face of Jesus in the many sacrifices their lives entailed. Don't judge by appearances. These simple folk are heroes in the eyes of God.

We often misjudge God's intentions as well. We haven't always focused the eye of the heart to discover the wondrous ways in which God is trying to woo us. We walk on blindly, unaware of the marvels of His understated expressions of affection. Maybe we don't pause enough in life to see beneath the daily hustle and bustle the supportive presence of God. In those occasional moments of quiet prayerfulness, we may catch a glimpse of His shadow moving alongside us. But Jesus, the Good Fisherman, is there. He is patient and clever. He knows how to bait the hook with what will lure our hearts

If we allow ourselves to pause in those moments of encounter with God, our hearts will joyously surrender. St. Augustine writes: "You called, shouted, and broke through my deafness. You flared, you blazed, you banished my blindness. You lavished your fragrance; I gasped and now I pant for you. I have tasted you and I hunger and thirst; you touched me and I burned for your peace."[35]

Our commercial society tries to sell us on the idea that more is better, that bigger is best. Success, fame, fortune — we are told — are what bring happiness. Didn't Jesus remind us, rather, that happiness lies in service, in sharing, sacrifice, forgiveness? Jesus wearied of the people's clamor for more signs and miracles, an appearance of flashiness and power. He generally prefers quieter, gentler ways of winning our hearts

Faith is the gift that allows us to see beyond the surface, beyond the appearance, and discover the substance beneath. The presence of God is there beneath it all. Humbly, Jesus comes to us daily, quietly hidden in the breaking of the bread. What the priest holds up appears to be bread and wine, but is truly the Body and Blood of Christ. Our faith in the real presence of Christ in the Eucharist is founded not only on Scripture, but also on the experience and faith of the earliest Christians, as well as the multitude of men and women who have carried the torch of faith down to our day.

As a young seminarian, I had a serious faith crisis concerning the Eucharist. Did those bumbling Apostles really believe that Jesus was truly present in the bread and wine of the Eucharist? They didn't seem to be that great at catching fish, how would they ever catch the meaning of these mysterious words of Christ? A fortuitous reading of the letters of St. Ignatius of Antioch showed me that, yes, the earliest of Christians really grasped that teaching in the same sense we do today. Ignatius, who succeeded Peter as bishop in the seaport city of Antioch, the city wherein the followers of Jesus were first called "Christians" (see Acts 11:26), is one of those great witnesses.

Due to the fact that he was one of the church leaders of his day, Ignatius was captured and sent off to Rome to meet his death in the coliseum. As did Paul before him, he sends a letter to the Christian community already formed in Rome pleading with them not to interfere with his scheduled execution when he arrives. He writes dramatically: "I plead with you; show me no untimely kindness. Let me be food for the wild beasts, for they are my way to God. I am God's wheat and shall be ground by their teeth so that I may become Christ's pure bread."[36] Martyred in the coliseum of Rome in A.D. 107, this letter of one of the earliest disciples reveals a dramatic belief in the real presence of Christ in the Eucharist, the Lord Jesus whom we discover "in the breaking of the bread" (Lk 24:35). When the priest holds up the bread and wine, don't judge by appearances. As the saying goes, "There's more to it than meets the eye."

QUESTIONS FOR REFLECTION:

1. How can I put aside my prejudices, my biases, and see others — the poor, the foreigner, the homeless — through new and humbler eyes, the eyes of Christ?

2. When relating to others, do I discern a tendency to behave like the Pharisee who misjudged the contrite tax collector? In what way can I correct that tendency?

3. How would I explain to others what the Eucharist means to me?

4. In what way has my reception of the Eucharist been an encounter with Jesus? Has it ever been like that sudden dawning of totally unexpected delight that the disciples at Emmaus savored?

Celebrating Discovery

CHAPTER 12

The Church as Community

Teodula's toothless smile could melt butter. Certainly it would melt your heart. Her life had been a hard one. She and her husband had been crop pickers on the American side of the border, migrating from lettuce fields in the Midwest to date palms in southern California. It was there that her husband fell from a tall palm tree and injured himself so that he could never do physical labor again. They returned to Mexicali and the husband spent the rest of his life begging on the streets. Their home was proof of their poverty. Whenever I visited their one-room house I was offered the only decent seat, while Teodula would sit on the bed or lean against a wall. The street outside was powdery desert dirt, which in the August showers would turn into *chickle* — gummy, gooey mud that was impassible.

The joy of Teodula's life had been their lovely daughter. Tragically, the daughter died at age eighteen. Teodula's strong faith got her through this pain, although I'm sure the daughter must have taken a bit of her mother's heart with her to the Lord. Whatever it was, this tragedy made Teodula's faith even stronger, even more joyful. She was the heart of San Francisco chapel.

Teodula would clang the church bell every day to summon people to Mass or rosary. She would lead them in prayer and song. Each week the youngsters would gather in front of her house for catechism. They sat outside the house on orange crates. Her "blackboard" was the backside of a metal Coca-Cola sign, bent and ragged, that someone had hauled out of the junkyard. Her teaching method was that of sharing romantic stories of the early Church martyrs, singing songs, and memorizing bits of catechism. The children and the parishioners all loved her as she had so much energy, enthusiasm, and that beautiful toothless smile. Probably the poorest person in that poorest section of the city, she was certainly the most beloved. Her faith, joy, and energy were the chief ingredients of weaving together these families into a well-knit community.

After all, that is what the Church is — a community, the people of God rooted in the person of Jesus. The people of God are never a neat, tidy, orderly, efficient gathering of sanctified saints. We come in our brokenness, some wildly liberal, others staunchly conservative, some saints, but most of us sinners. Pretty much like the first Apostles — confused, bewildered, slow learners, churlish at times, foolishly eager at other moments. We aren't much different than those small Christian communities in Galatia and Corinth that St. Paul founded and later needed to write letters chiding them for their petty rivalries and bickerings.

The church is not a gas station where we drive in, fill up with gas, get a lube job, have little contact with anyone else, and drive off good for another 3000 miles. The church community is not impersonal, antiseptic, and sterilized; rather we are called to rub elbows with one another, to interact with people whom we might prefer to avoid. We may hate the music, want to avoid giving the sign of peace to some stranger on our right, want to dash out at the earliest moment so we can get out of the parking lot more readily. But we cannot pretend we love God if we don't love our neighbor, as unpleasant as that fellow might be, as sloppily dressed as she might appear.

We may want to have a relationship just with Jesus and not have to be bothered with those around us. We may be crying out interiorly, "just leave me alone." Hurt by what others may have said of us, crushed by the ways in which loved ones have let us down, rejected, or betrayed us, we prefer the safety of the inner harbor of our own ego; we'd rather take shelter on the protected side of the breakwater than face the stormy seas of human relationships. But the Lord reminds us that we are called to reach out, to be Christ to one another. Such is the hard reality of life. If we are anxious to find Jesus, it is not just in the Eucharist or in our prayers that we must look for Him, but in our neighbor, our friends, and yes, in our enemies. "For he who does not love his brother whom he has seen, cannot love God whom he has not seen" (1 Jn 4:20).

We want sermons that will make us feel good, tell us we are loved. We are uncomfortable, if not angry, when the preacher rants on about what we think are political issues that don't belong in church. "Just talk to me about a loving Jesus," people will tell me. I once had spent a few weeks in Central America during the tense era of the Sandinistas. When I returned, the pastor of the parish where I had at one time served and been much loved asked me to share my experience with the parishioners. I decided to take the approach that people from the Christian community in Nicaragua had urged me: "Just tell them what the Catholics of Nicaragua would like to share." So I did. After a few minutes into my homily I noticed that about a third of the people were getting up and leaving. I glanced around thinking maybe there had been an earthquake and I hadn't noticed it. Then I realized it was because of my preaching that they were heading for the exits. My stomach churned in pain, my face blanched in embarrassment. It was a horrible feeling to experience such stark rejection. At each Mass I tried different ways of softening the message, stressing the fact that very often political issues are moral issues as well and that the Church needs to address them. I suggested they might ask whether or not God himself wasn't messing in politics when He ordered Moses to lead His suffering people from Egypt. Wasn't that loss of cheap labor going to cause Pharaoh great economic problems? Wasn't God himself mixing religion and politics? Jim Wallis, in a *New York Times* editorial, comments, "The separation of church and state does not require banishing moral and religious values from the public square. America's social fabric depends on such values and vision to shape our politics — a dependence the founders recognized."[37] Generally, though, we prefer hearing about the Jesus meek and mild rather than about the angry Jesus tossing the moneychangers out of the temple. We prefer the consolations of God to the challenges of God.

There is also a part of us that prefers to find God in the extraordinary rather than the ordinary, in the glamorous and not the hand-me-down simple moments of daily life. We look for the transcendent, lofty presence of God in the great cathedrals of the world, often failing to see His immanent presence in the quiet lives of our work-a-day world. We dream of a trip to Lourdes or Fatima, not realizing that spending quality time with our own family or a lonely neighbor might be a way of discovering a subtle, but equally miraculous healing presence of God. We might long to see the wounds of Jesus depicted on the shroud of Turin and forget the wounded in our own neighborhood, even in our own family.

The endeavors of creation, crucifixion, and redemption are not static, one time only events. They are ongoing activities, creative moments in which God wants each member of the community to grab a shovel and pitch in. When Jesus raised Lazarus from the dead, Lazarus came out of the tomb bound in his shroud of linen bands. Jesus could easily have approached his old friend and loosened the bands himself. But rather He said to those standing about, "Unbind him" (Jn 11:44). That is what He asks us to do, to unbind one another of the anger, the prejudice, and the fears that imprison us. He invites us to be involved with Him in the work of healing and forgiveness.

Even those who feel helpless can minister. How? By letting us minister to them. I recall a simple, loveable man, José, who lived not far from Teodula, on the same dusty street. He had lost his wife a few years earlier. They had had no children, so José lived alone. He had suffered from diabetes and his legs were both amputated right at the hips. José's house was also a one room house, about 12 feet by 15 feet in size with only a bed and a wheelchair resting on the dirt floor. A heavy rope hung down from a rafter — like a hangman's noose — just above his head, so that he could grab hold of it to lift himself up to a sitting position and chat with visitors. The only other room in his house was an adjoining store front only about six feet in depth in which he had his little display of candies and a Coca-Cola cooler. He operated his modest store on a trust system. The neighbors, who all revered José, would come and help themselves to the food, leaving behind enough cash for their shopping that would enable him to make a little profit.

> **The separation of church and state does not require banishing moral and religious values from the public square.**
>
> — Jim Wallis

Often in the evening a few men would gather around, wheel José out under a tree and play dominos with him. I'm sure Jesus was there in the shade of the palm trees, looking on with a big grin on His face.

It takes people working together with the Lord to build a community. In earlier centuries when the craftsmen toiled at building a mighty cathedral they would place gargoyles on the walls and rain spouts — humorous, grotesque, devilish figures — that would mock the efforts of the artisans, reminding them that such a gigantic and sacred undertaking was no mean task. Our cooperation with the Lord in the ongoing construction of the new kingdom means much effort and disappointment before the task is completed. But such is the struggle of giving birth.

The principle work of the church community, however, is not in its acts of charity and various ministries, but first and foremost in the performance of liturgy, particularly the Eucharistic liturgy, in which Christ becomes uniquely present. The liturgy of the Eucharist is the source, the oasis of grace that gives us life and enables that life to blossom into budding ministries. Since liturgy is the work of the community it must be participative and understandable. But yet it must remain, in a sense, a mystery. I think I can better explain this by using the example of the role of the icon in the Eastern Church. I learned about this from the Russian Orthodox in Alaska. The Russian Orthodox were the first missionaries to work with the various groupings of Eskimos in southwestern Alaska in the 18th century, and the native Aleuts and other Eskimo groups of this area remain loyal to them to this day.

We of the Western Church may well be struck by the difference of artistic style of the icon from western art, as well as by the devotion shown to icons by the Orthodox. When we of the West admire a religious painting we admire it as the creative achievement of a particular artist — the warmth of a Giotto painting or the gentle delicateness of a work by Fra Angelico, for example. The Eastern Church, however, takes quite another view of the role of the individual artist. Most of the Orthodox ecclesiastical painters have remained anonymous. The making of icons is a sacred craft practiced in monasteries. The procedure of painting itself is a liturgical act, with a high degree of holiness and sanctification of the painter. Much as a bishop of the Western Church fasts and prays before consecrating a church, the painter-monks prepare themselves by fasting and penances. Brushes, wood, paints, and all the other necessary materials are consecrated before they are used.

Ernst Benz,[38] in *The Eastern Orthodox Church*, explains that the Orthodox theologians do not interpret icons as products of the creative imagination of a human artist, but rather a true epiphany, a self-made imprint of the celestial archetypes. And so, interestingly, the icon is a two-dimensional painting, a mirror image of a sacred person. It is not the image that is the object or the recipient of veneration, but the archetype that "manifests itself" in it. To look through the window of the icon is to look straight into the celestial world. Consequently, there is a sense of awe we experience in venerating the icon, a sense of the mystery of God that is bigger than an individual painter's ability to express, and so it is expressed in this symbolical, liturgical reflection somehow incarnated in it by God.

The liturgy of the Eucharist, in its own way, must carry a sense of mystery and awe about it. We do not use tortillas and Coca-Cola as the elements of the Eucharistic meal, even though they are more popular and common than unleavened bread and wine. But the latter are timeless symbols of the eternal hunger of humankind. Although the liturgy must be made understandable so that we can participate in it, it must also be balanced by reverence, by sacred silence, by use of candles and incense that mark this off as a special moment, a moment similar to what Moses experienced at the burning bush. It is more than a casual prayer service.

As Eamon Duffy,[39] in his fascinating work *The Stripping of the Altars*, points out, in the middle centuries of the history of the church, a screen was built to partially block the view of what the priest was doing during the central part of the Mass. Although in the twelfth century the custom of the priest elevating the consecrated host came into practice so that people might gaze lovingly on the host, by the fifteenth century the custom of a rood-screen came into existence, a decorated frontispiece that partially concealed the altar and priest. During Lent, moreover, a huge veil was suspended on weekdays within the sanctuary area, to within a foot or two of the ground, completely blocking the laity's view of the celebrant and the sacred action. Both screen and veil were barriers, marking boundaries between the people's part of the church and the holy of holies. The purpose was to emphasize the sacredness of place and Eucharistic presence, but an unfortunate result was that people were so awed by their nearness to sacred ground that no one dared approach it to receive Jesus in the Eucharist. Adoration rather than reception became the primary purpose of the Eucharist, overshadowing the fact that the food of the Eucharist is what nourishes us on our journey to and with God.

In those years before Vatican II, as some may recall, that main part of the Mass, although now somewhat more visible, was said secretly in silence and with the priest having his back toward the people. In addition, the recitation of Mass in Latin, which most people did not understand, kept a mysterious air about the liturgy. And so I find it interesting that even though the Mass is now in English, and we may clearly understand what each spoken word means, we still don't really grasp what is happening. That is fine, because we would be foolish to think we can comprehend the incomprehensible power and love of God. It is by faith that we know that Christ becomes present. It is beyond our understanding, because it is the manifestation of a love that is too deep for us to grasp with our mind, and only in some imperfect way with our hearts.

The apex of liturgical celebration within the community is that of the Easter Vigil. Let us briefly look at that.

John the Evangelist makes a stunning revelation — *the crucifixion was not about death but about birth.* John's Gospel was written many years after the death and resurrection of Jesus and the community has had much time to reflect and understand more profoundly the meaning of all this. As a consequence, John paints a portrait of a Jesus who is not a victim but an active participant in launching the new kingdom. His pain on the cross and Mary's anguish are like birth pangs. In His last breath, Jesus breathes forth the Holy Spirit. Like the grain of wheat, Jesus has died and new life is born in and through the creator Spirit. A new and better creation is now launched. The blood and water that flow from Christ's side after being pierced by the sword represent baptism and Eucharist, the headwaters of new life.

This is what the Christian church celebrates in the drama at Easter, the drama that is called the paschal mystery, for it was initiated at the Paschal (Passover) meal. It is a drama in three acts: the Paschal meal, the death, and the resurrection. Holy Saturday night's vigil is the highlight of the drama. Like a great symphony by Mozart, the new and better creation is celebrated by pulling out all the stops of symbolism, and employs sacramentals that speak to all five of our senses. The blessing of the fire and water symbolize the primordial elements of nature, the lighting of the paschal candle represents Jesus, the new light of the world. We process into the darkened tomb of the Church, receiving lit candles, reminders of our call to pass along the torch of faith. In dark silence, we hear the account of the first creation, its being scuttled by the first shipmates, and God's determined plans to do it again. We even resort to sexual symbolism as the paschal candle is plunged three times into the new water as part of the blessing ceremony. A new and better life is conceived. Neophytes are dunked into water and oiled up with chrism to remind us that baptism calls us all to join in God's "Habitat for Humanity" project. The bombastic singing of the "Gloria" as the Church lights are illuminated and candles lit ushers in this exotic new creation. It is new in that Jesus launches this new covenant between the Father and His people at an intimate last meal wherein He opens His heart to His followers, and in the deepest witness of love — the giving of his own life. It is better because we are invited to actively cooperate with Father, Son-made-visible, and Spirit in the on-going process of creation, healing, and sanctifying. The Easter vigil is high drama, the highlight of the liturgical year, the still point around which all love, all creation, revolves. The celebration of the Eucharist is a celebration of discovery, proclaiming that Christ is indeed present, not only in the Eucharist, but in the word of the Scriptures, the priestly celebrant, and the people gathered in worshipful, faith-filled celebration.

It is people like Teodula and José, the salt of the earth, whom Jesus calls to give birth and nourish the building of a community, to hand on the torch of the faith, to serve as the coworkers of God's construction crew. Leaders of the community may not always be those with the highest degree or most eloquent speech, but those with the biggest heart and most joyful soul. They may be the steelworker down the street, the teller at your local bank, your neighbor who is always borrowing your lawn mower or cup of sugar. "Blessed are the poor in spirit, for theirs is the kingdom of heaven" (Mt 5:3).

QUESTIONS FOR REFLECTION:

1. Fr. Rolheiser compares participating in the liturgy of the Eucharist as being one member of the orchestra in a concert. I need to put my own personal preferences aside for the greater good of the orchestra. In what way does personal prayer differ from the Eucharist, which is the communal, symphonic prayer of the Church? Are both types of prayer needed? How can I accomplish both, or can I?

2. Pope John Paul II writes in an encyclical on Sunday worship that the Mass does not end with the final blessing, but in going forth and sharing what I have received at the Eucharistic celebration. In what realistic, practical ways can I accomplish that?

3. Some of us remember the days when we went to church to "hear" Mass. Now we are asked to participate actively and knowledgeably in the liturgy. What are my reactions to the present manner of the communal celebration of the Eucharistic liturgy?

4. An elderly priest advises in *The Diary of a Country Priest*: "The Word of God is a red-hot iron. And you who preach it 'ud go picking it up with a pair of tongs, for fear of burning yourself, you daren't got hold of it with both hands."[40] What scriptural passages are too hot for me to handle?

CHAPTER 13

Rooted in Christ

The little four-seater plane clipped the tops of the pines as we eased over the last ridge of the mountains. The plane bounced gently as it landed in a field where a group of about ten Tzeltal Indians were waiting for us with horses. Bishop Samuel Ruiz, two other missionaries, and I got out with our overnight packs and road horseback for a few miles. We reached a small river and climbed aboard several dugout canoes. I had always thought "dugout canoe" sounded so romantic. I was taken aback to discover they were basically burly mahogany tree trunks about 15 to 20 feet in length, hollowed out by machetes, the center burned out with fire, and the inside smoothed up by hand ax.

The natives ferried us a mile or so to their village downstream. We were floating through the garden of paradise! Colorful jungle birds flitted about in the trees, entertaining us with their songs. The smell of countless wildflowers wafted through the air. Large branches of wild orchids draped from the trees almost to water level. Admiring the beauty of the orchids, I observed that these orchids do not put their roots into the earth, but rather into the tree. It is from the tree itself that they draw out their nourishment and sustenance.

The orchid inserting itself into the tree offers a fine metaphor for being "rooted in Christ." By rooting ourselves in Christ a spiritual transfusion takes place by which we imbibe the very lifeblood of Christ, transforming us that we be compassionate, effusive in our love, and concerned for justice, as is He. Even though life brings its moments of struggle and pain, by inserting our roots in Christ and receiving life from Him, we experience peace and joy knowing He is faithfully with us at all times. This peace is not something superficial, nor the type the world sees as merely a freedom from worries; it is the fruit of purification. Its soil is a broken, humbled heart; its harvest is a disciplined, ordered mind.

The holy person is a wholesome person, a person of joy. True religion is not guilt centered, but joyful, because it is Christ-centered. There should be lightness about the Christian life, an exuberance and cheerful spirit. "Make a joyful noise unto the LORD" (Ps 100:1), says the psalmist. St. Thomas comments on our need to ease up, "lighten up," as we say today: "Unmitigated seriousness betokens a lack of virtue, because it wholly despises play which is as necessary for a good human life as is rest." On the other hand, I've never been comfortable with the expression "We are an Alleluia people," as it seems too naïve; it too easily overlooks the reality of human suffering. The joy of Christ is not giddiness, but the result of understanding that God is with us in both our moments of grief as well as those gentle moments of lighter winds.

> The measure of one's love for God depends upon how deeply aware they are of God's love for them.
>
> — Diadochus of Photice

Joy is always celebrated by sharing food and drink. We throw a party to celebrate an occasion; we have a formal dinner to honor a guest or mark a special milestone in life. Scripture describes the ultimate intimacy with God as an "eternal banquet." The metaphor, however, has always come across to me as a little flat. I have attended banquets that were stiffly formal and confining, people dressed in their most elegant and least comfortable clothing, seated next to someone they barely know and may never meet again. I find a more colorful visual in what the Mexican calls a *convivencia*, a joyful, informal coming together to share food, song, and good company. It rather resembles an

American potluck, but with the added warmth of songs similar to the ones we used to sing around Boy Scout or Girl Scout
campfires. The warmth and camaraderie bring a sense of peace
and joy, a sense of belonging. I have a hunch that Jesus would
have added to the warmth of such a joyful experience and not
sat sulking stern-faced in some corner.

Jesus is often pictured as a pretty somber and serious fellow.
Certainly the awesome responsibility of being the redeemer
Messiah was a serious and somber task. But I'm sure there was
also a lighter side to Him. Don't the Gospels portray Him as a
person who loved to be with people, to join them for meals? In
his fine book, *Dining in the Kingdom*, Fr. Eugene Laverdiere
reflects on the ten meals Jesus had with various groups as nar-
rated in Luke's gospel. Jesus must have been delightful to be
with. Would people have given up all they had to follow Him
if He were grouchy, lacking spunk and humor? Wasn't it more
likely that He would have had a magnetic personality, a catching smile, and a friendly gleam in His eye? He tells the joke on
himself that people called Him a wine bibber always eating with
sinners (Lk 7:34).

Also in Luke's gospel we witness His enthusiasm as He
rejoices with His novice Apostles at how well they had fared on
their first foray "fishing for men" (see Mt 4:19 and Lk 10:17-19).
Or I can see Him with a big smile on His face, chuckling a bit,
as He looks up at Zacchaeus clinging awkwardly to the branches
of a tree to catch a better look at Him. He must have laughed
as He said, "Zacchaeus, make haste and come down; for I must
stay at your house today" (Lk 19:5). An invitation to friendship
cheerfully extended.

Even His style of preaching and teaching was homespun,
reminding me a bit of the stories Abe Lincoln would spin to
make a simple point that politicians often obfuscate by their
political polemics. Fr. Albert Nolan writes:

Nothing could be more unauthoritative than the parables of Jesus. Their whole purpose is to enable the listener to discover something for himself. They are not illustrations of revealed doctrines; they are works of art which reveal or uncover the truth about life. They awaken faith in the listener so that he can "see" the truth for himself. That is why Jesus' parables always end with an explicit or implicit question which the listener must answer for himself.[41]

As He did with His disciples, Jesus calls us to share His friendship. Friendship is an experience of shared joy, a moment of awesome beauty, a treasure for life. Friendship with Christ truly encountered, evanescent as it might seem at times, is a breathtaking instance of awe and wonder, a gentle awakening to the sacredness and richness of life. This friendship that makes of our life something beautiful is nourished, as are all friendships, by sharing time together, opening ourselves to one another.

God knows of our unique beauty because He has knit us together in our mothers' wombs and knows well the potential for goodness and creativity that is there. In the prayer of quiet, God gently allows the clouds to part briefly and illumines for us His beauty in His awesome presence and as it is flushed out in one another, in the events of life, and in the word of Scripture. This awakening to beauty is like the tide that gently rises in all the coves and inlets along the shore, bringing in new life and gifts. Among those gifts is a deeper awareness of the beauty and goodness He has deftly sown within us.

Haven't we all been humbled when someone fell in love with us, yet feared the day they would discover we were indeed but earthen vessels, presuming that they would move on to look elsewhere for friendship. But John tells us that God first loved us, and He loved us in our sinfulness, already aware of our foibles. The more we can accept that love, the more we grow. Guilt is not enough to change us. I have always felt, for example, that the challenge to drug addicts — "Just say 'no'" — was too simplistic. Before we can say "no" we have had to say "yes" to something, to have chosen life, and to see that our dependence on drugs destroys that possibility. All our promises, pledges, and resolutions fail, because the motivation should not be that we are failures, but that we are loved, and nothing is more transforming than love.

Responding to the invitation to be rooted in Christ is risky business as well, and nudges us out into a relationship with God; it may prove hard for us to fathom the depth and mysterious paths of this relationship. A fifth century bishop writes:

> Anyone who loves God in the depths of his heart has already been loved by God. In fact, the measure of one's love for God depends upon how deeply aware they are of God's love for them. When this awareness is keen it makes whoever possesses it long to be enlightened by the divine light, and that it seems to penetrate their very bones. They lose all consciousness of themselves and are entirely transformed by the love of God.[42]

Western Christendom, with its emphasis on the Fall and its after effects, focuses on God's goodness in the moment of Redemption wherein Christ buys us back from eternal ruin. Eastern Christendom, on the other hand, places its emphasis on our "deification," the invitation from God to share in His intimate life. A very meaningful symbol is carried out in the course of the Mass, which admirably captures this miraculous blending of God and ourselves. It is a symbol of our deification, our call to share the very life of God. At the time of the offertory, the priest pours into the chalice the wine that becomes the Blood of Christ at the Eucharistic celebration. Then he lets fall a few drops of water into the wine. The water represents us in our lowliness and frailty; the wine signifies the richness and beauty of God. When the two are mixed together, the water disappears. It has become one with the wine, indistinguishable in its oneness, much as a little tributary flows into the greater river and is no longer visible in its separateness and smallness, but has become one with the great river as it moves towards the sea. The two elements have become one. While performing this action the priest offers a quiet prayer that has woven into it the words of St. Irenaeus, one of the great teachers of the Church of the fourth century: "As this water is mixed with the wine, so may we participate in the divinity of Christ who came to share in our humanity." The symbol points to a reality deeper than can be expressed in words. At our baptism, God breathes into us His very Spirit and we share the divine life of God. That spirit burns within us, transforming us like spun gold, that we grow more and more like unto Christ, and make Christ visible and present in the world so that by our values, life, and actions, we are Christ made present for the glory of God and the building up of His Church, the people of God.

We have been called to participate in the very life of God. This idea is very hard to fathom, for it is so extraordinary. We are swept up into the very bosom of God's life, but we seem to live as though it were only a dream, not a reality. The symbol of the mingling of water and wine represents our call to deification, to be God-like. Not to be gods, but to realize the sacredness of human life, to not just love God, but to love "as God loves." The Eastern Church has stressed this truth with greater energy than the Church of the West. I admit to having preached too often on correcting poor behavior, encouraging leading a better moral life, but not reflecting sufficiently on this profound truth of the indwelling of God, forgetting the philosophy of St. Thomas Aquinas: *agere sequitur esse*, "what we do flows from what we are," such as a healthy tree bears healthy fruit. We of the Western culture are more action minded; we focus more on doing than being. We preach moral correction, but must balance that with a deeper awareness of the dignity of being incorporated into the intimate life of God, the indwelling within us of the Trinity. We tend to see our entering into eternal life at the moment of death, rather than at the moment of our baptismal birth. We are already in the realm of eternal life. We have already begun our life with God, knowing that if we are faithful to it we will later experience it in its fullness. Like entering the narthex of the magnificent cathedral of Chartres, anxious to move into the main part of the church and drink in the beauty of the stained glass windows flooding the vast nave with its flowing rainbow of colors, we stand here and now within the entry way to eternal life, preparing ourselves for splendors of which the mind has never dreamt.

How is it, though, that we go about rooting ourselves in Christ? First, of course, it is by the grace of God. Your very desire to be rooted in Christ is already a gift from God. But the workings of the Spirit require our participation and cooperation. I would say that a prime requirement is developing a faithful life of prayer. We need a daily contact, a frequent opening of our heart to the Lord. It does not much matter which form of prayer you prefer, the important point is to set aside time each day to share your heart with God.

Each of us has our rhythm of work and daily habits, so only you can determine when and how much time you can set aside. Our response may well be, "But I'm so busy, and I have have no time." Or, as I myself used to be inclined to claim, "my work was my prayer." But I found that was not really sufficient. The commitment of making time for prayer is a concrete way of making God a serious priority in your life. Secondly, I find good spiritual reading important as a way of helping me appreciate the special beauty of the Scriptures. Keeping informed on how we ought to understand more fully our response to what John XXIII used to call "the signs of the times," the current problems and needs of today's society, also reminds us that our light is not to be kept under a bushel basket.

Furthermore, there are times when we need serious fasting and penance, times when we find ourselves struggling with one or other robust temptations, or moments in which we have hit a patch of listlessness, or notice that, as with the law of gravity, our interest in our beloved Jesus has begun to sag a bit. When the Apostles found that in certain cases they were unable to cast out evil, Jesus told them those are the times we need especially to fast and pray. Those are the times we need seriously to put our shoulders to the wheel, and as hard as it might be, I have found that the Lord will indeed come to our aid.

Another way to facilitate your being rooted in Christ is in remembering your baptismal call. When you were baptized, the priest anointed you with sacred chrism and challenged you to be "like Christ: king, priest, and prophet." How are you to be "king"? As we mentioned already, by realizing your dignity as a child of God, recalling that you have royal blood flowing in your veins. Therefore we are to treat others and ourselves with dignity and respect, acknowledging each of us as a member of God's beloved family, a membership that is more important than our nationality or race of lineage. We are to be priests in the sense that we are called to make our world sacred and beautiful, to be willing to make sacrifices to engender love in our society. Finally, we are called to be prophets, which means to live that faith with courage and joy. This is the vocation of each baptized Christian; being rooted in Christ is the source of our enabling power, and our rootedness is made stronger therein.

Beauty is the surest proof of the reality of God. The glint of love in the beloved's eye, the light shimmering on the gently rippling waters of the bay, the gurgling sound of the infant wriggling in his crib, the sweet fragrance of citrus in bloom; beauty wooing the heart, beauty discernible in the multifarious manifestations of life, reflecting the infinite imagination of the creative spirit of God. Who can doubt there is a God as he watches a mother lovingly cradle her newborn child in her arms?

Like orchids stealthily slipping their roots into the rich juices of the tree, or the redwood pushing its roots further down searching deftly for water at deeper depths, we too join in that search as we root ourselves into God's inmost being. Touching God, joy breaks forth and blossoms into exuberant, new-born life. Wisdom and courage are conceived.

> I bow my knees before the Father, from whom every family in heaven and on earth is named, that according to the riches of his glory he may grant you to be strengthened with might through his Spirit in the inner man, and that Christ may dwell in your hearts through faith; that you, being rooted and grounded in love, may have power to comprehend with all the saints what is the breadth and length and height and depth, and to know the love of Christ which surpasses knowledge, that you may be filled with all the fulness of God (Eph 3:14b-19).

QUESTIONS FOR REFLECTION:

1. In what practical, concrete ways can I go about being more fully rooted in Christ?

2. At what moments have I experienced changes in values, actions, or my very being that were results of this being rooted in Christ?

3. In what Gospel passages have I seen humor or warmth in Jesus, saw a lighter side of Him that made me feel at ease rather than guarded with Him?

4. In what concrete ways have I experienced sharing in the divinity of God?

CHAPTER 14

Wonder and Worship[43]

The culmination of the liturgical year is the great feast of Christ the King. This cyclical recalling of the story of our relationship with God down through the ages reaches its final turn on this last Sunday before Advent. Our intimate history with God from creation, through the fall of Adam and the consequent preparation for the Messiah, redemption, and final judgment are reviewed and relived from Advent to the glorious ending on this feast of Christ the King, the patronal feast of the King Islanders. King Island is a tiny island in the narrow Bering Strait that divides Alaska from Siberia. The U.S. Government no longer allows anyone to live there because it is so remote and inhospitable. For many years, though, the Eskimos inhabited this island living off the seals and whales they hunted. The Jesuits provided heroic missionaries who dwelt on this treeless rock and ice formation, missionaries who learned the native language and shared the very difficult and isolated life of their Eskimo parishioners. During the cold war a large statue of Christ the King was placed on top of the craggy island, pointing toward Russia, symbolizing our prayers for their conversion. (Maybe it is time to turn the statue around to face ourselves!)

Each year, the few remaining King Islanders gather at the morning Mass at Holy Family Cathedral in Anchorage to celebrate their patronal feast. They sing proudly in their guttural native tongue, many dressed in their native kuspics. The drum is the sacred music of the Athabascan Eskimo. Their drum is a simple hoop with a seal skin stretched taut over the wooden frame. The beat is a steady, slow beat. As a King Island Eskimo told me, it is to remind us of the first sound we humans hear

— the sound of our mother's heart thumping as we lay warmly nestled in her womb. The beat is sacred and fills us with joy and wonder at the greatness of God's nature. In honoring our mother who gave us life, we honor the God of love and life.

The Mass is a celebration of joy and wonder. Joy by its nature is diffusive of itself, bubbles over to infect others with its warmth. We experience a burning need to express in word or action the joy that is in our hearts. God Himself longed to speak a word of joy to us. Jesus is that expression. He is the Word made flesh that makes visible the invisible love of God for His creation. A little child gleefully shares with her mother a card she made at school. A husband comes bounding into the house to share the news of his promotion at work. These persons would feel crushed if, having arrived home, there were no one there with whom to share this gift. Grief, as well, needs another's shoulders to help bear its heavy burden. We are social animals; we need others with whom we share our hearts, as did Jesus with Mary, Martha, and Lazarus.

James Carroll once put it so beautifully: "Our world will not be wonderful until we ourselves are full of wonder. We have this cherished need to push beyond the limits of the ordinary, to discover what belief and hope claim is there — a mystery place of awe and true communion."[44] However, when we encounter the beautiful, experience the inexpressible, are awed by the grandeur of God, or overwhelmed with love, we need to resort to imagery, story, parable, poetry, or silence to express what cannot be put into words. When I say to a beloved friend, "I love you," the words fall short of what truly is in my heart. Lacking words, we revert to other forms of expression, such as sacrament and symbol, to point to a reality that is bigger than human vocabulary and imagination can manage.

Liturgy and sacraments are ways by which we mark off moments of special encounter with God in our lives, moments of wonder and worship. This custom of celebrating special places and occasions is ancient. Sacred time and place are the longitude and latitude of our spiritual world, by which we can chart and navigate the journey of our liturgical life. The anthropologist Mircea Eliade describes the way in which people in the earliest cultures went about building their homes. For these ancient civilizations, to build was to re-create, to do on a small scale what God had done on a larger scale in creating the universe. Thus it was a sacred event. Accordingly, the couple would invite the priest to their plot of land and he would divine at what point on their land a straight line could intersect unimpeded with the center of the world. He then would insert his sacred pole into the ground at that location, and the hut would be built around it. It would be built in such a way that a large opening would be left in the roof so that the angels could ascend and descend through this opening, much as we see in the story of Jacob's ladder in the Old Testament. The ancients viewed God as yearning to share their home, their world, with them.

One of the earliest devotions of Christians was the pilgrimage. Psychologically and spiritually, the pilgrim relives the biblical Exodus, a difficult journey to an unknown world. The journey is meant to be one of growth, of being formed, as were the Hebrews, so that the pilgrim would be open to God's will and directions. As the Hebrews, they needed to trust that their leader knew what he was about, even though at times they lacked food and seemed to be going in circles. The pilgrimage is the symbol of our spiritual journey, our being formed, hammered, and shaped by the Holy Spirit, learning to trust in God as He leads us through green pastures and arid deserts. The Church itself is on pilgrimage to the heavenly Jerusalem and is depicted as the bark of Peter transporting us across the sometimes heavy seas of life.

Processions are pilgrimages on a small scale. I recall well the processions of the Blessed Sacrament through the neighborhood when I was a child. This type of Eucharistic procession was very much in vogue in the 14th century. In England, for example, people would prepare for it a whole year in advance, much as southern Californians today prepare for the Rose

Parade. Villages, trades, and unions would vie for the best and biggest float. This traditional way of honoring the Eucharist was the most celebrated day of the year. The procession is an important symbol. Admittedly, it is very hard to concentrate and pray attentively while processing, especially when, as in Mexico, fireworks are being set off, children running about, and dogs barking from all the commotion. The importance is to help us realize that, indeed, our life is a pilgrimage with the Lord and reflect on what that means, and by this public act of faith challenge others to reflect on it as well. The need is precisely to realize we are indeed needy, to acknowledge that, just as the procession, we must have a goal so that life makes sense. The Christian is one who has owned the saying of St. Augustine, "Our hearts are restless until they rest in you, O Lord." We find salvation in surrendering to our God, and, as Chesterton puts it, "We not only feel freer when we bend, we actually feel taller when we bow."

Yet as wonderful and beautiful as is this marvel we call creation, there is a mushroom cloud that hangs over it. Evil, indeed, is present in the garden. Some of us recall the radio program "The Shadow," which would begin with the chilly introduction: "Who knows the evil that lurks in the hearts of men? . . . The Shadow knows." There is something lurking out there that wants to destroy the creation that God called "good." As Eamon Duffy comments, "Our society is informed by a sort of hectic glee at the discrediting of virtue, the defiling of the holy: we love to be told that nothing is sacred."[45] Although St. Thomas Aquinas philosophically describes evil as the lack of good, a flaw in existence, evil is a very concrete, powerfully existing reality that wreaks havoc in God's creation.

I recall Fr. Louie sharing with us how he went out one day on horseback to celebrate Mass in one of the native villages in our parish in Chiapas. Somehow he confused the location and unknowingly took the wrong trail and ended up in a village that had turned itself over to devil worship. Unwittingly, he headed for the small chapel and a few curious village women came in.

He proceeded to celebrate Mass, but at the moment of elevating the host, he said that literally all hell broke loose. The ladies screamed and wailed and dashed for the door. Somehow they had witnessed a clash of the power of evil with the power of Christ in the Eucharist.

Not all evil is as dramatically explosive as that. We need to realize the devil is a wily and clever opponent and that rather than dramatic evil possessions and Hollywood style pyrotechnics, the devil prefers the subtle attack. Like a clever general he will feint and distract us, then when we have been sucked into the trap he closes in from the other side. He will tempt devout persons to go for a lesser good and thus gently start them off on the downhill road. Less astute people will be tempted to do the right thing for the wrong reason. A sixth century hermit wisely remarks on the devil's tactics: "For when the devil looks at a man who sincerely desires not to sin, he is not so unintelligent as to suggest to him (as he would to a hardened sinner) that he go and commit fornication or go and steal. He knows we do not want that and he does not set out to tell us something we do not want to hear; but he finds out that little bit of self-will or self-righteousness, and through that, with the appearance of well-doing, he will do us harm."[46]

> **Our world will not be wonderful until we ourselves are full of wonder.**
>
> — James Carroll

In our American society we cherish freedom of opinion. But soon we find that truth becomes relative and irrelevant. If you want to believe the world is flat, that's fine with me. If you want to believe that the Eucharist is just some vague, generic presence of Jesus as in the statement "where two or three are gathered in my name, there am I in the midst of them" (Mt 18:20), that's fine. But the truth is, isn't it, that it can't be both ways: either the world is flat or round, either Jesus is in the Eucharist, Body, Blood, Soul, and Divinity, or not. Either the wall facing you is there or not. It's only by getting up and walking face forward into it that you will find which is the truth. So, staking everything on this principle of freedom of opinion can lead us into erroneous and unfortunate results if we do not support it with checks and balances. Truth is not a subjective feeling, but a correspondence of what is in the mind with what is in outward reality. Truth is not easy to come by because of our own biases as well as the difficulty of seeing reality objectively in all its many facets. Pilate's question, "What is truth?" (Jn 18:38) was a very insightful one.

The same is true of morality. The breakdown of family life isn't just the result of a good thing finally rusting out. Insisting on our first amendment right of freedom of speech, the media has progressively flaunted a greater portrayal of violence and immorality, and as a consequence all young people believe that there is something odd with you if you haven't had sex before marriage, or, if you're married, that you've not chalked up at least one wild adventure on the side. Vengeance and violence is portrayed as the only response to misunderstandings. Unrestrained freedom can lead to unmitigated license and dehumanizing behavior. The devil does not need to resort to dramatic, frightening appearances when such subtle undermining erodes the underpinnings of society.

The recent scandal in the Church of priests molesting children is a further tragic example. I doubt very much, from my own experience working in religious formation in the seminary, that these men entered with any other motive than wanting to serve the Lord and His people. They would not have endured if they had come for reasons any less deserving. But somewhere along the line they must have experienced loneliness, a hunger for love, an emotional or sexual immaturity, a disorientation of their inner spiritual compass, and dehydration of their prayer life. Somehow the devil found a flaw in their innermost heart and bent it toward a cancerous sexual aberration. Did they realize their lives were out of control? The cancer spread and affected a larger segment of clergy and religious than anyone imagined. Tragically, it is precisely we who are supposed to be His faithful servants who have reopened the wound in the side of Christ, and it will take a long time in the healing. Generations will pass before the people of God once again have confidence in their shepherds, before the voice of the Church will achieve credibility.

Finally, we can see the work of the evil one undermining the values that build up and make a healthy society. The increasing aggression of country against country, the deepening gulf between wealthy and impoverished nations, the increasing disinterest in reaching out to the poor, and the undermining of marital and family life directly work against the call of the Church to build the kingdom, to work for a world of peace, justice, and love.

St. Peter judiciously advises us, in a verse that is used in the official night prayer of the Church: "Be sober, be watchful. Your adversary the devil prowls around like a roaring lion, seeking some one to devour" (1 Pet 5:8). We see in Luke's Gospel that Jesus begins His public ministry by being led by the Spirit itself into the desert to meet the devil head on. Even though Jesus outwits and rejects the devil, Luke reminds us that the devil will come back at a more propitious moment to try again. That moment, of course, is the kiss of betrayal by Judas that sends Jesus on the ghastly road to Calvary.

A few of us may remember the humorous line: "The devil made me do it." But in some sense the real evil is within us and needs to be exorcised by prayer and fasting. One of the desert fathers said, "Our own wills become the demon and it is these which attack us." Each one of us has our addictive habits that need to be faced in some type of twelve-step program, some process of conversion of heart. We are all, as Henri Nouwen stated, wounded healers. Acknowledging that is one of the steps in becoming poor in spirit, pure in heart. It is not an easy truth to own up to.

So the battle between good and evil, between beauty and the beast, goes on. Reminiscent of an earlier cinema era, in the book of Revelation this battle with the beast ends when Jesus comes riding in on His white horse to slay the foe! That's the battle between light and darkness that we relive during the final three days of Holy Week and dramatize at the Easter vigil. In the long run, good wins out over evil, Jesus by His death and resurrection gives birth to a new kingdom that replaces what Adam and Eve lost in their original sin of pride. Therein lies our hope, the confidence that God can bring forth good from evil, and therein lies our joy because the new creation is better than the original one, for in God-made-flesh we see the face of love, compassion, and forgiveness. The Preface of the second Eucharistic prayer for reconciliation describes how this is achieved:

> In the midst of conflict and division, we know it is you who turn our minds to thoughts of peace. Your Spirit changes our hearts; enemies begin to speak to one another, those who were estranged join hands in friendship. And nations seek the way of peace together.

So it is that the liturgy of the Eucharist is the source and goal of all worship. It is Christ in the Eucharist that satisfies the eternal hunger of the human person for life and love, Christ who joins in our struggle for growth and wisdom and who nourishes us in turn to be bread for a hungry world. We enter into it with reverence; we are urged by the church to be present "by conscious, active, and faithful participation." The beautiful prayer of St. Thomas Aquinas describes it well: "O sacred banquet in which Christ is received, the memory of His passion recalled, and the pledge of future glory is given to us." Past, present, and future gathered into one unifying moment of prayer and praise. It was in the breaking of the bread that the disciples recognized Jesus in the village restaurant in Emmaus, the same bread that gives us life today (see Lk 24:13-35).

I write these words while seated less than 100 yards from the gentle Iliuliuk River in the Aleutian Islands. At this moment there are thousands of salmon energetically swimming their way upstream to the point they themselves were born where they will lay their eggs and die. Their decaying bodies will be the food for their offspring. No one knows how the salmon, having spent several years in the ocean, are able to navigate their way back to their original source. This sacrificial act, this ritual dance, is accomplished on pure instinct. Christ does the same for us, but out of pure free will; out of love He died for us and nourishes us with His very Body and Blood that bring life eternal.

I have had the privilege of sharing the Eucharist in the jungles of Chiapas, in the frozen climes of Alaska, in St. Peter's basilica, and in sun-baked fields in Mexicali. Each was an experience of mysterious encounter with the sacred, each was an attempt to express the human hunger for love and meaning, encounter and intimacy. The hunger of God's love for us and our hunger for Him meet at the table of the Lord. There, wonder becomes worship. Like the disciples journeying to Emmaus, we recognize Jesus in the breaking of the bread. Partaking of that bread we also recognize Jesus in the broken of the world.

QUESTIONS FOR REFLECTION:

1. The human person has a need to express what is important to him or her in liturgical actions. What are some "liturgical actions or rituals" that I have seen displayed at colorful activities such as sports events, civic celebrations, or political conventions?

2. What does this hunger for liturgical expression teach me about our hunger for beauty, for meaning, for expressing the inexpressible?

3. A minister once boasted that his church was not one "of smells and bells." How is it that my experience of God and my worship are enhanced by the use of my five senses? How do sacramentals such as holy water, candles, and incense help me to touch the untouchable, reach the unreachable?

4. Evangelicals often accuse Catholics of being idolaters because we "adore the wood of the cross, idolize pictures of saints, and make Mary more important than Jesus." How might I respond to those accusations?

Lost and Found

CHAPTER 15

The Humility of God

I quietly watched her from a distance as she gently fanned the leper lying on the old army cot. This part of the leprosarium was the least kept up. It was where the worst patients were kept. Not many wanted to view them. The building was an old army barracks clumsily rebuilt after World War II. Cockroaches scurried about the floor in search of crumbs. The humidity was heavy and steamy. Slowly, she waved the large fan over his body, naked except for a small loincloth. The man, her husband, was frail and wasted away. The ears and nose had been eaten away by the leprosy, the eyes filmed over white, the legs and body rotting away from the dread illness. She stayed faithfully at his side. No one would have blamed her if she were to abandon him and seek out a new life back in Manila. I was watching Jesus heal the leper. My heart was numb.

"God with us" is Jesus' name: "Emmanuel." God has seen the suffering of His people and has come to speak to us of who He is. In Jesus we see the compassion, the patience, the total self-giving of the Father. Seeing is believing. In Jesus, God is made visible, tangible, audible. "Listen to Him" (Mt 17:5, Mk 9:7, Lk 9:35), spoke the voice of God to the Apostles at the transfiguration. How does Jesus speak to us?

"And the Word became flesh and dwelt among us" (Jn 1:14). The spoken word is like a sacrament — the outward expression of the inward heart. Profanity is so destructive because it reveals the meanness of a person's heart. Swear words always demean what is most sacred: God, love, intimacy. Language should be something sacred, emanating from the good will within us. Jesus is the perfect expression, the echo of the Father's total loving goodness.

There are various ways of speaking. We can express what is within us by word or symbol, by gesture, by silence, by deed. We also speak through body language. If you are giving a homily or teaching a class and notice eyes glazing over or heads nodding, you know you are in trouble. If you are speaking with someone and he is squirming about, you know he is nervous and not at peace.

Jesus is God's body language — word made flesh. Let us listen to what He is saying. First, amazingly, that He is helpless, vulnerable. Nothing is more helpless than a newborn baby. The child lying in the feed trough in Bethlehem is none other than God himself. His helplessness wins our hearts. Here, the creator of the stars and seas lies helpless before the smelly shepherds. Isn't that precisely what love is — surrender, a willingness to be totally open to the other, totally vulnerable to rejection and betrayal? Love is risky business.

> **Jesus is God's body language — word made flesh. Let us listen to what He is saying.**

Isn't that what Jesus experienced? "He came to his own home, and his own people received him not" (Jn 1:11). Even prior to His birth He experienced rejection: "There was no place for them in the inn" (Lk 2:7). Rejection followed Him through life. Rejection by the religious leaders, the people of His own hometown who wanted to push Him off the cliff, even by His own relatives who thought Him mad. The same was true for His death. "Jesus, your Son, innocent and without sin, gave himself into our hands and was nailed to a cross," we pray in the first Mass for Reconciliation. An attempted embrace twisted back upon itself. Love betrayed.

Ironic, isn't it, that the all-powerful God allowed Himself to be so powerless and vulnerable. The first three centuries of Christianity witnessed many people who could not accept that

Jesus was truly man and God, because they could not believe that God would allow himself to be so grossly insulted. Yet, down the ages emperors and conquerors have fallen and their memories become covered with the dust of ages. It is the person on the cross who has proven victorious. His vulnerability — the vulnerability of love — has conquered our hearts more than anyone else. His naked poverty on the cross speaks more convincingly to us than the royal robes of mighty potentates.

This decision to enter quietly into the world was a conscious decision on God's part. Remember that after Jesus' baptism at about age 30 the Spirit led Him into the desert and there He was severely tempted. Tempted to be Jesus Christ Superstar, tempted to wield His power for the glory of His people, to trample down the foe and make of Israel a mighty nation. That was the reason that some of His disciples chose to follow Him, seeking those hoped-for glory days. Jesus chose, however, to conquer with the power of humble love. We can see that this temptation had been and still remained a struggle, for when Peter later chides Jesus not to speak of going to Jerusalem to be crucified He hits a tender nerve. Jesus responds brusquely, "Get behind me, Satan!" (Mt 16:23, Mk 8:33).

St. Thomas Aquinas has this magnificent passage:

> There is here something else inflaming the soul to the love of God, namely divine humility... For Almighty God subjects Himself so much to each single angel and every soul exactly as if He were the purchased slave of each, and any one of them were his own God... now, such humility results from the wealth of divine goodness and nobility, as a tree is bowed down by its plentiful fruit.[47]

It is in humility that God wins our hearts. That pathetic figure on the cross epitomizes the depth of God's mad love for us. In God's speaking to Hosea the prophet, relating how He will lead His people into the desert and there will woo their hearts, we see an Old Testament image of this humility. How humbling that is for us to hear, for we are so aware of our own unworthiness, our faults and sins, yet He wants to woo our hearts! We do not need to prove ourselves to Him, but rather to surrender to Him and let Him draw forth the goodness in us by helping us shed all that is not Christ-like within us.

We, in our turn, are a word spoken by God. The person living out a life of grace and faith gives glory to the Lord, makes the voice of Christ audible in the marketplaces of the world. God can point to you and say, "This is My body." We, the members of the Church form His mystical body. Because we are a body, though, we at times fail. We anguish over the shame the Church has faced in recent times. Yet the Church has weathered even worse times, when the popes themselves were the cause of suffering and embarrassment. There are those times when the Church used its power not to give life, but to maim and kill in the name of religion. We are earthen vessels, used in our weakness to show the loving power of God. Having feet of clay, the mystical body of Christ, guided and energized by the Spirit of God, must always be renewing and renovating itself. In some type of balancing act, God seems to raise up some of the greatest saints, such as a St. Catherine of Siena or a Mother Teresa, precisely at a time when some of our more embarrassing figures take the scene. Kathleen Norris wisely says:

> The Church is like the Incarnation itself, a shaky proposition. It is a human institution, full of ordinary people, sinners like me, who say and do cruel, stupid things. But it is also a divinely inspired institution, full of good purpose, which partakes of a unity far greater than the sum of its parts. That is why it is called the body of Christ.[48]

Secondly, Christ manifests His power in His humility. As we reflect on the helplessness and humility of a God who lies in the Christmas manger, let us be aware that it is precisely this aspect that gives love its power. Jesus is born in a feed trough to remind us that He has come to nourish that deep hunger within each of us; He comes as food in the Eucharist to strengthen us for the journey of faith. Let us be aware that if we let the child Jesus transform us into other Christs, it is precisely through our willingness to risk loving our enemies, our neighbors, and ourselves that we are most able to give life to the world and fill the darkness with light. There is no love without risks, without sacrifice. Only in a humble use of the power of love are we strong enough to overcome the power of hatred.

Basket weaving is a sacred art for the women of the Aleutian Islands. The finished products are very expensive, as much time and love go into their making. A person could purchase a straw basket in a modern department store for only a few dollars, products of mass-production, sterile results of modern technology. The Aleut woman takes great time and care in selecting from the tundra the suitable plants and strands. She develops the skill in determining the times for soaking and drying them. A child being trained in this art begins by learning special songs to be sung, for the artist must woo and honor the strands that they be supple in the artist's hands. Much experience is needed to acquire the proper ability to weave the strands together so that the pattern does not bunch up here or drift over there. Each artist creates her own patterns and style that distinguish them from other Aleut weavers. Like the priest lifting up the offertory gifts, the artist lifts up to God the simple materials the Creator sowed in the field now transformed and transfigured in her song of praise, her completed, crafted vessel of love and beauty.

We are the simple grasses of God's good earth, and we too must be humble and supple that we be gracefully pliable as the divine artist weaves us into the warp and woof of His new creation. It is to Him to select the wheat from the chaff, to stretch us and enfold us, to choose the design and the outcome. It is to us to be pliable and trusting so that in our simple goodness His presence may be transfigured in the weaving of a world that enfolds in its open basketry the gifts of peace, justice, and consequent joy.

> Have this mind among yourselves, which was in Christ Jesus, who, though he was in the form of God, did not count equality with God a thing to be grasped, but emptied himself, taking the form of a servant, being born in the likeness of men. And being found in human form, he humbled himself and became obedient unto death, even death on a cross. Therefore God has highly exalted him and bestowed on him the name which is above every name, that at the name of Jesus every knee should bow, in heaven and on earth and under the earth, and every tongue confess that Jesus Christ is Lord, to the glory of God the Father (Phil 2: 5-11).

QUESTIONS FOR REFLECTION:

1. What are some of the qualities of God's personality that have won over my heart?

2. Humility enabled Mary, St. Francis, and Bl. Teresa of Calcutta to be joyful, life-giving, creative persons. Who are some of my friends or contemporaries that I see possessing that same quality?

3. In *The Brothers Karamazov*, the monk, Fr. Zossima, says: "A loving humility is a terrible power, the most powerful of all, nothing compares with it."[49] Have I experienced humility as self-pity, or as fertile ground for growth? How has it empowered me?

4. When I am humbled by my failures, in what ways am I able to recover a sense of hope and worthiness? How can I use my brokenness to rebuild my friendship with God?

CHAPTER 16

Through the Eyes of Compassion[50]

◡‿

This particular Sunday was no different than any other summer Sunday at *Nuestra Señora del Rosario* parish in Mexicali — scorching hot, people milling around finding shelter in a bit of shade in the patio fronting the church, ladies selling tasty Mexican food and fruit juices in front of the Church to raise money for the parish. A young man parked his battered pickup alongside the church and came to me asking if I would bless the body of his child before he went to bury her. I asked where the body was — thinking it was at his home — and he told me it was in the front of his truck. Taken aback I accompanied him to the street. As he pulled a little homemade box the size shoes come in out of the front seat, he said that the child had died at birth. I quickly invited those who were standing around to accompany me, and, at my urging, the young father carried the little box to the church. We placed it on the altar. Everyone gathered around as I said a blessing over the baby and together we said a few prayers and ended with a Marian hymn. I struggled to find something helpful, something consoling, to say to the father. I wish I could have said as Jesus did to the royal official whose son was ill, "Go; your son will live" (Jn 4:50). Befuddled, all I could think of was, "It looks like she's gone home before you. She'll be waiting there for you."

Most funerals in Mexico take place within twenty-four hours of death, as embalming generally does not occur, certainly not in the case of the poor. The young man carried the child off and drove out to bury her at the foot of *el Centinela*, "the Sentinel," a 2000-foot mountain whose skirts flirt with the U.S. border. A "do-it-yourself" cemetery is there for the poor families to bury their dead. Hundreds of white crosses, some flanked by plastic flowers, others overwhelmed by tumbleweeds, are nestled there in the sandy, rocky soil, not in neat rows, but scattered haphazardly as space and boulders allow. Care is needed to bury the bodies deep enough to discourage the coyotes from digging up the remains. Each time I would drive past this desert final resting place for the poor, I would think that as ironic as it sounds, Jesus is most present here. As Jacob had said after wrestling with the angel, "This is none other than the house of God, and this is the gate of heaven" (Gen 28:17).

In some sense, this child who never witnessed the rising of the sun, heard the chatter of the ravens, watched a sea otter frolic on its back, is mourned because it died a virgin in the experience of earthly life. It never saw the sparkle in a beloved's eye, the mist mingling in the tops of the redwoods, a flaming orange sun settle into the ocean's horizon, nor heard the song of the whippoorwill. Yet, some might say it was blessed for that fact. I have known parents who decided not to bring children into a world so frightful and violent. Might we say, rather, that it is blessed, not for what it missed, but for what it gained so early, and be heartened therein? For this child took a direct flight from here to eternity, with no stopovers to delay its arrival. Hasn't it immediately experienced the glory, grandeur, and beauty of an enamored God, frolicked in the sumptuousness of the Almighty's garden? Hasn't this child, rather, seen the twinkle in the creator's eye, whereas we have only seen His hand in the glory of creation? Hasn't this child heard the angels sing, witnessed the Spirit sending forth its multifarious transforming graces, whereas we have caught but glimpses and hints of God's tenuous presence among us? Hasn't this child prayed for its parents — and they for the child — that they one day make the final turn on the road toward home and know in a moment of intense intimacy the beauty of their child in a deeper way than they would have known had she walked with them sixty years? When we arrive home, it will be our loved ones who arrived ahead of us that will be there to welcome and tour us about a Disney-land Walt Disney never dreamed of.

Death is a two-sided coin: at once a farewell and a welcome home. Here, we only experience the farewell side at that metro station we call death. We who remain behind clutch dearly the memories and photos of our beloved. But they who exit here and clamber aboard God's train and continue on homeward bound will experience a welcome greater than Times Square offers its heroes. I'm sure that, like our family who have gone before and longingly await us, yes, this child will be there to welcome home its father, he who in tears, amidst cacti and tumbleweeds, buried her earthly remains. "Why do you seek the living among the dead? He is not here, but has risen" (Lk 24:5).

> **Compassion is hard because it requires the inner disposition to go with others to the place where they are weak, vulnerable, lonely, and broken.**
>
> — Henri Nouwen

On the other hand, we who remain behind do not always find life to be one great Disneyland. One need only read some of our American writers of the middle of the last century, authors like Carson McCullers, Flannery O'Connor, or John Steinbeck, to be reminded how heavy and burdensome life can become. In many ways these are the type of people Jesus seemed to relate to so well: the poor, the rejected, the marginalized. I am sure, for example, Jesus could easily identify with Rosa Parks. Remember the story? It had been a hot, sultry day in Montgomery, Alabama. Rosa Parks was weary, her feet hurt, and she just wanted to find the first seat on which she could rest her tired body. She clambered aboard the bus. The front seats were empty. A few of her brother and sister African Americans sat sweltering in the back rows. All those empty seats right there in the front of the bus wooed her and she yielded and just sat down there bone tired, not able to push her energy further. Gruffly, the driver hollered at her, "There's no room for you there. Move to the back where you belong." She stayed seated. And thus began a revolution.

I believe it is with that same drift of meaning that Luke tells us "there was no place for them in the inn" (Lk 2:7), when Mary and Joseph are hastily attempting to find a place for the child to be born as the mother's contractions were coming more frequently. "There was no place for them." I came to a new understanding of that on an occasion in which I accompanied Bishop Samuel Ruiz out to the Chiapas jungle for an ordination of lay deacons. Six native men, one from each surrounding village, were to be accompanied by their wives and be confirmed in the role of leadership. There, out in the jungle, a larger type of hall had been constructed some years before basically of some supporting pine wood poles and siding of palm fronds and banana leaves. The dirt floor building served as classroom, church hall, and catechetical center. This particular night it was to serve as the inn for all the guests coming for the ordination. The bishop and I each found a place on the ground to put down our bedrolls and stretch out. As more and more people came, we would all adjust and move closer. There was always room for someone else. It struck me then that this is most likely the way inns were operated in the time of Mary and Joseph. There was no Motel 6 or Ramada Inn in those days that would put up a "No Vacancy" sign when they had filled to capacity. There was always room for one more. When Luke says there was no room for them in the inn, the meaning is more like what was addressed to Rosa Parks: "You are not wanted here." Jesus' entry into our world was met with rejection. His death was an unjust, ungrateful, unmerciful rejection.

Wherever there is pain, loneliness, injustice, hatred, failure, rejection, poverty — Jesus is there. Whenever we experience any of this, Jesus is there sharing the burden with us. He had such great plans for us and met with what seemed total rejection and failure. But His reaction was not, "Father, slay this motley, ungrateful hoard," but "Father, forgive them; for they know not what they do" (Lk 23:34). He came and hung there naked for us, stripped of all dignity. He took the risk of love, of giving all, knowing that it may only be used against Him. But isn't it His hanging there that indeed and in fact has won our hearts? The crucifixion goes on. Whenever we suffer in some way Jesus suffers, the body of Christ suffers. But also the resurrection continues. When we share these sufferings with the Lord, they become part of the healing of the world, in their odd way they change our hearts and bring us to a deep awareness that God is with us in our struggles. His embrace from the cross heals us and bestows on us a deeper life and peace. Jesus gives us the eyes of compassion, and with Him we look out from our crosses to a suffering world and discover the hidden presence of God in that enormity of aching hearts. However, compassion is not an easy virtue. This is what Henri Nouwen has to say:

> Let us not underestimate how hard it is to be compassionate. Compassion is hard because it requires the inner disposition to go with others to the place where they are weak, vulnerable, lonely, and broken. But this is not our spontaneous response to suffering. What we desire most is to do away with suffering by fleeing from it or finding a quick cure for it. As busy, active, relevant ministers, we want to earn our bread by making a real contribution. This means first and foremost doing something to show that our presence makes a difference. And so we ignore our greatest gift, which is our ability to enter into solidarity with those who suffer.[51]

I learned that very lesson one afternoon as I was going into the cathedral in Mexicali to see one of the priests. There, near the main entrance, was a cripple sitting on the sidewalk begging. I was tempted to drop in a few coins and be on my way. Something moved me to sit down beside the man on the grungy sidewalk. I had never done that before, never stopped to see the beggar as a person rather than an object of charity. I simply asked him how he was, gave him a chance to share a little of who he was. I realized that giving a little of my time to him was giving him some dignity, acknowledging that he indeed was a fellow traveler, a human being with his joys and worries just like me. Then I realized that this is exactly what God did, He "became flesh and dwelt among us" (Jn 1:14), or, as another translation has it, "He pitched his tent among us." He sat down beside us.

Several generations ago, before I was ordained, I helped out one summer at an enormous dumping ground for the sick, the maimed, and the insane lumped together in a facility euphemistically called the county hospital but resembling more the state prison. The chaplain, a priest encroaching upon senility, had a heart of gold, a brave warrior attempting to bring some cheer to the employees and patients of this financially deprived facility. I became infatuated with a young patient about my age whose life had become a nightmare. Shortly after her marriage her husband took her hunting. Little did she know she was the object of the hunt. From a distance he shot her in the back and left her for dead. However, she survived, paralyzed for life from her neck down. Lying there in the hospital she would have to be rotated every few hours in an attempt — which ultimately failed — to prevent bedsores from forming. She shared with me the panic that would attack her when flipped over on her stomach, her faced pressed into the pillow, struggling to breathe, unable to move her head or even to cry for help. Her bed was only one of about forty, lined side by side in a long, barracks-like dormitory, each patient worse off than the next. I visited her every few months, but eventually faded out of the picture as a wheelchair patient from the men's ward developed a friendship with her. I wasn't steeled enough yet to deal with this kind of suffering, couldn't offer anything other than limp platitudes, was shocked to see mental patients chained down because left to their own devices they would pound their heads against the walls. The mind recalls what Moses warned God the

Egyptians would say if, in His anger, God would smite His people after all they had gone through in the desert — in effect, "Where is your God now?" (see Ps 115:2).

Don't we all entertain similar thoughts when we see the parents at a children's hospital clinging to hope as the doctors try one treatment after another, but each time the hope they cling to gets further diminished. We experience it when we reflect on the misery of life in jail, the sadness of the poorer old folks homes, orphanages, cancer wards. "Where is your God?" I don't think there is a solid philosophical, metaphysical, rational response. I don't condemn those who wretch when they hear pious inanities, or simply lose their faith, for the only answer is the folly of the cross. Who could believe that God would be so foolish to seek out death in the most hideous fashion known, the pain of having flesh stripped from His body by scourging, tolerate hanging naked before His mockers. Yes, our God is there — not just in the dedicated nurses and doctors, the scientists in their far off labs searching for a cure — He is there in bed with the patient, experiencing the same pain, the same struggle, but now as the comforting angel similar to the one the Father sent to strengthen Him in Gethsemane. He accepted the foolishness of the cross to portray with those bold strokes and powerful colors of a Rouault painting the intensity of His love. Only love can be so mad, so sacrificial. Maybe that is what the mysterious "sin against the Holy Spirit" (see Mt 12:32, Mk 3:29, Lk 12:10) is about — not being able to grasp the length and breadth and depth of God's love. "Then he said to Thomas, 'Put your finger here, and see my hands; and put out your hand, and put it in my side; do not be faithless, but believing'" (Jn 20:27).

QUESTIONS FOR REFLECTION:

1. Let me list some of the times I have tasted the compassion of Christ or of others.

2. What opportunities have I had to share in another's suffering? What have I learned from their personal sorrows and sufferings?

3. When I am visiting a sick person, or someone lonely, am I aware that I am being Christ made visible to them, that my loving presence is more important than any words I may say?

4. How do I respond when I am asked why do bad things happen to good people?

CHAPTER 17

The Good Fisherman

The majestic mountains of Montana kept the hectic world at bay. Tucked away in a serene valley just north of Yellowstone Park, with its azure blue lake, we did our best to lure a trout to catch his breakfast so that we might later enjoy him for dinner. They must have been on their guard that day, as it was only after many casts that Fr. Kieran finally guided a lovely trout into his net. A much more skillful fisherman than I, he said, "Let's open him up and see what he's been eating." The thought had never crossed my mind, but this old fishing pro knew what he was about. As he opened the entrails he shouted gleefully, "grasshoppers." So we spent about twenty minutes catching grasshoppers to use as bait. They were a taste delight to the gullible trout. We had marvelous success.

In a sermon to some Dominican nuns along the Rhine, the German mystic Eckhart speaks of God's clever fishing skills:

> God lies in wait for us with nothing so much as love. Love is like a fisherman's hook. Without the hook we could never catch a fish, but once the hook is taken the fisherman is sure of the fish . . . Therefore wait only for this hook and you will be caught up into blessing, and the more you are caught the more you will be set free.[52]

Jesus is the Good Fisherman. He knows how to bait us. He knows what will attract us, what logs we might hide under, what eddies we might use to dart away. On one hand, we want to be caught up into love; on the other, we don't want to lose our independence and freedom. How badly we want someone to love us, to hold us special, to be the one that makes their heart throb, their eyes sparkle; and yet, anxious about surrendering what we think is our freedom, we dart hither and yon to escape the bond of love. We see that in the classical "calls" in which God summons great persons to lead His people, their response is also a dodging of that invitation: Jeremiah says he is too young, Isaiah says he is unworthy, Moses says he has a problem with stuttering, Peter says, "I am a sinful man, O Lord" (Lk 5:8). And when push comes to shove, don't we too stall and dodge, settle for a comfortably balanced Christianity that won't rock our boat, not push our guilt button. Jeremiah, after yielding to God's call, later repents and in anguish says, "O LORD, thou hast deceived me, and I was deceived" (Jer 20:7). Or, as we might say today, "You duped me, Lord, and I let myself be duped." How did I get myself in this mess? Haven't you experienced often that when some people come back to the Church to serve in one fashion or another things suddenly fall apart for them — someone gets sick, another loses their job — and they too cry out, "You duped me, O Lord."

Why is it that we hesitate? What is it that holds us back from a full surrender to God? I think it is because we know deep down in our gut that if we swallow hook, line, and sinker our lives will change. And we don't really want that. There is something in me that wants to cling to my self-centeredness, an awareness that if I am fully converted to Jesus I will need to be forgiving, self-sacrificing, nonjudgmental, forbearing, and all those other qualities that will challenge me to grow beyond my comfortable little world. Deep down inside me, I rather sense that if I really get the treasure Jesus calls us to pursue I won't be able to cling to it like a child who won't let go of his prized toy so his sister or brother can play with it. We somehow know that the key to finding the treasure is in being dedicated to sharing it, to sharing the love Jesus has given me with those whom He calls me to serve in deed and example. Love, like Mary pouring out the precious oil on the Lord's feet, is precisely increased in our unselfish willingness to generously pour it out without counting the cost.

But then, that is what it is to be poor in spirit, pure in heart. It is that quality of dispossessing myself of clinging to my own needs and preferences and discovering in that a surprising freedom and peace. So it is true, "the more you are caught, the more you are set free." That is the irony of being open to God's transforming love. I suppose if a caterpillar were a rational animal it would hesitate going into its cocoon with the same fear we have of yielding fully to God. For little does the caterpillar know that this dying to oneself is what allows it to be transformed into something beyond its wildest imagination.

We read in Luke's Gospel how Jesus caught His first disciples at the Lake of Gennesaret. After a long and fruitless night of fishing, Jesus encourages them to "put out into the deep and let down your nets for a catch" (Lk 5:4). Peter at first protests, but decides, what the heck, give it a try. Swamped to the gunwales with the fish they marvelously caught, they had to holler for help from another boat. On docking, Jesus invites them to follow Him. No protests now. No begging time to straighten out the nets, clean the fish, put the boats in order. "And when they had brought their boats to land, they left everything and followed him" (Lk 5:11).

Jesus invites us to step out in faith, to go out into the deep with Him. It is an invitation to intimacy. It is the intimacy we hunger for, because it is an intimacy we know will never be betrayed, an intimacy that will calm the storms of life, that will take us out into the depths of the immense love of God. The human friendships and love that God provides us with throughout life are reflections and sharings of the love He has for us. A love that comes to us through human beings is true, God-given love and needs to be celebrated as such. Henri Nouwen reminds us that:

> God has given you a beautiful self. There God dwells and loves you with the first love, which precedes all human

love. You carry your own beautiful, deeply loved self in your heart. You can and must hold on to the truth of the love you were given and recognize that same love in others who see your goodness and love you.[53]

That striving on our part to shake loose the hook that has snared us is the process, the spirituality, of becoming poor in spirit, of leaving behind our hankerings for other loves, other pleasures, other glories, so that we may glory fully in the love God hungers to share with us. Yes, God hungers for our love. Incredible. In the new basilica of Our Lady of Guadalupe in Mexico City, there are various enlarged photographs of the *tilma* — the outer garment — of Juan Diego on which was miraculously imprinted the image of Mary. One photo is a highly enlarged photo of the eyes of Mary, and in the pupils of her eyes can be seen the reflected image of Juan Diego to whom she was speaking. Just as our names are written on the palms of God's hands, so our image is reflected in the pupils of His eyes. We pray with the Psalmist: "Keep me as the apple of the eye; hide me in the shadow of thy wings" (Ps 17:8). How much more intimate could a relationship be?

What was the bait Jesus used to catch Peter and his fellow fishermen? Possibly for some it was the excitement of the moment, for others a longing for fame, for others maybe just curiosity. How did Jesus catch you? Was it a sense of guilt, a nudge from a friend? Was it a feeling of peace, a desire to be of help to others, the joy of working at Jesus' side? Was it, as in the case of Augustine of North Africa and Anthony of Egypt, that a line from the Gospels was the zinger that stopped you short? Only God, who knows the inner highways of your personality, the paths of your genes, the depths of your heart, is shrewd enough to know whether it will be a moment of anguish or an experience of joy that will woo your heart. But once you are caught, His hope is to develop a deep friendship with you, a friendship that will open undreamed of vistas for you.

Friendship, whether with another person or with God himself, launches us onto a path of transformation, a process of becoming more mature, more responsible, more whole. We may discover, however, how hard it is to put the other person first, to put his or her needs and wants ahead of our own. We may discover new facets of the other's personality — and they of ours — and find that it may be difficult to adjust and accept them. God, too, can become more demanding of us than we had planned on. We liked it better when everything went smoothly; when we felt the compassion of God rather than the challenges of God. In our struggle to be Christ-like, we find God takes us in directions we weren't prepared to go. We are pushed to make sacrifices we hadn't counted on, and we are reminded of the fact that "My thoughts are not your thoughts, neither are your ways my ways" (Is 55:8).

> **God lies in wait for us with nothing so much as love.**
>
> — Meister Eckhart

Hopefully, though, your journey with Jesus will be the joy of your life. Some can date this friendship back to early childhood days, a simple, uncomplicated friendship, nourished by their parents' faith, strengthened by simple prayers. The growing pains of teenage years were made bearable because the unseen Jesus was felt close at hand. Sometimes the embarrassments and disappointments caused us to question whether our friend was still there, or wonder, as did Teresa of Ávila, why God treats His friends so shabbily at times.

As the friendship develops and life goes on, we grow in our trust of God as we in turn take on more responsibilities. At times, though, life becomes more hectic, and we may find that in our busyness our daily contact with Him has weakened or even temporarily vanished. We may even find that we have wiggled free of the hook. But he somehow catches us up again. Like the prodigal son, humbled and chastened, we return to our ever-faithful friend.

Elizabeth Barrett Browning asks, "How do I love thee? Let me count the ways." Jesus shows us the ways in gentle epiphanies. So gentle and subtle that we often fail to notice. Yet the Lord is there, transparent, in the ones we love, the blessed events we experience, and He is obliquely present in difficult times and trying persons. He shows His love by His faithful journeying with us from when He knit us together in our mothers' wombs and on through our growing in the Spirit until that day He brings us face to face with the Father. In that journey, He lives out His role as the Good Shepherd, protecting and guiding us. In the course of our pilgrimage to our true homeland, God will keep us from being bored by playing hide and seek with us, appearing in one disguise or another, now delightfully present, later cleverly hidden. Should we get discouraged and be tempted to turn back, the Good Fisherman will suddenly appear in some comical, unexpected way, such that our pulse will begin to beat faster and the joy of the hunt will captivate us once again. We do not journey alone; we are all members of one family. Graced by the Spirit, bolstered by the companionship of the Lord, we cheer each other along in our ongoing game of discovery.

I would like to share a few lines from a treasured poem entitled "The Flight in the Desert," by former Br. Antoninus, O.P., an old friend, crafter of words, and novice of mine at the time.

> This was the first of his goings forth into the wilderness
>   of the world.
> There was much to follow; much of portent, much of
>   dread.
> But what was so meek then and so mere, so slight and
>   strengthless,
> (Too tender, almost, to be touched) — *what they nervously*
>   *guarded*
> *guarded them.* As we, each day, from the lifted chalice,

that strengthless Bread the mildest tongue subsumes,
to be taken out in the blatant kingdom,
where Herod sweats, and his deft henchmen
riffle the tabloids — that keeps us.[54]

In a special way Jesus is visible in "the lowly," the ones who get served carp rather than trout, the ones who wait in interminable lines at the bus station or the welfare office. It was their faith, patience, and fresh cheerfulness despite the calamities of life that motivated me to find a more compassionate and less juridical, judging Jesus. They spoke to me of a warm-hearted, affable companion, ever faithful, ever supportive.

Many years after that fishing venture in the pristine forests of Montana, I went fishing with Don Ramon one afternoon in an irrigation canal in the searing heat of Mexicali. Murky, unhealthy dregs of the Colorado River oozed slowly along. We had no fancy flies, no shiny reels. Just a 10-foot long net. Jumping into the canal with all our clothes on, we stretched the net taut between us. Tennis shoes on so that we would not cut ourselves on broken glass bottles, we waded chest high through the dirty water. After about 100 yards we stopped and lifted the net out and sorted out what we had collected: sticks, frogs, beer cans, and a few garbage-eating carp. We took the fish to Don Ramon's home, barbecued them in his dirt yard, and shared the catch with his seven children. The feast was beautiful in its simplicity. Husband and wife, seven children, and myself munching on bony, burnt fish. I felt Jesus' presence there with us, warmed by the same joy He experienced early that morning a few days after His resurrection when on the shore He barbecued the fish for His bewildered Apostles. That memorable morning when, between bites, He looked at His old friend Peter and asked, "Do you love me?" (see Jn 21:15-17).

That is the same question He puts to you and me.

QUESTIONS FOR REFLECTION:

1. In what ways do I dodge or put off the call to friendship with God?

2. How do I explain to a friend what Eckhart means when he says, "The more you are caught, the more you are set free"?

3. John says in his gospel that it was four in the afternoon (or the "tenth hour," see Jn 1:39) the day he felt the call of Jesus. What is the moment I first felt God's call to friendship?

4. What are some of the high and low moments of this friendship? Has this relationship teased bounteous joy from my weary soul, given me eagle's wings, been the love that makes my world go 'round?

EPILOGUE

The colonial city of San Cristobal de las Casas, Chiapas, is a lovely mixture of old tile-roofed buildings and white-washed homes resting tranquilly atop the mountains. Much of its importance lies in the fact that it is here that "international law" had its roots. Its first bishop, Bartolomeo de las Casas — for whom the city bears part of its name — was shocked by the treatment the Spanish conquerors, the *conquistadors*, imposed on the natives. The conquerors not only stole the land from the Indians, but even made them slaves on what formerly had been their own few hectares of coffee or corn. They tortured them, killed them as thoughtlessly as swatting flies. Bishop Bartolomeo was incensed at this outrageous treatment, but the Spaniards replied that these people were subhuman. And so Bartolomeo took up his mighty pen to challenge this injustice. He recruited as cohorts the Dominican bishop in Nicaragua, Antonio Montesinos, and the Dominican missionaries who accompanied to Peru the most atrocious of all the conquerors, Juan Pizzaro. In the mid-sixteenth century, they began writing to the Dominicans in Salamanca, Spain, which at that time housed one of the more important theological schools in Europe. They wrote these Dominican theologians asking them to plead the Indian's cause to King Charles V of Spain and his successor Philip II.

Francisco de Vitoria, O.P., took a particular interest in this cause, and at his insistence the king did pass laws stating that the human rights of the Indians were to be respected. Unfortunately, because of the enormous distance of Spain from its new colony, there existed no efficient way to enforce those laws. Fray Francisco Vitoria became the first serious writer and thinker to inaugurate modern international law. He claimed that the government of backward peoples, such as the Indians appeared to be, might legitimately be taken over by a more enlightened state — in this case Spain — *provided it was for the welfare and in the interest of the former, not merely for the profit of the latter.* This was the principle of the system of mandates that was established after World War I.

Pope Leo XIII in 1891 was the first pope in our era to seriously address social and political issues. He sought to bring the Church into dialogue with the modern world, but also challenged that society to live up to the standards of the Gospel in terms of social justice. Some Church historians consider his encyclical *Rerum novarum,* "Condition of Labor," to be the most important papal pronouncement ever. From that time on, each succeeding pope has written forceful encyclicals on social justice issues. More recently, the American bishops have added to those writings by their own frequently composed pastorals on particular issues facing our country. Sadly, these encyclicals and pastorals, as well as the whole of Catholic social teaching, are as unknown as was the Person of the Holy Spirit before the charismatic movement rediscovered Him. These encyclicals are often critical of our American way of life that has been affected in many ways by values inherent in capitalism and materialism.

The *Catechism of the Catholic Church* continues to spell out its anxiousness that we pay attention to matters of justice, a concern that is one of the main themes of the whole Old Testament. The *Catechism* states:

> Respect for the human person entails respect for the rights that flow from his dignity as a creature. These rights are prior to society and must be recognized by it. They are the basis of the moral legitimacy of every authority: by flouting them, or refusing to recognize them in its positive legislation, a society undermines its own moral legitimacy (cf. John XXIII, *PT* 65) (CCC 1930).

Our concern must be for any and all injustices committed against the human person from conception to the grave. As Cardinal Bernardin once observed, the issue of life is like a seamless garment. Justice plays a very important role in the Old Testament. The king was supposed to rule like God himself, that is, with concern for justice for all. If he abused his power it was the task of the prophet to confront him or any other group that abused human rights. Laws were formulated to protect the widow, the orphan, and the alien who normally would not have any rights. In Deuteronomy, we find a theme that is repeated frequently in the Bible, that of compassion: "When you reap your harvest in your field and have forgotten a sheaf in the field, you shall not go back to get it; it shall be for the sojourner, the fatherless, and the widow; that the LORD your God may bless you in all the work of your hands . . . remember that you were a slave in the land of Egypt; therefore I command you to do this" (Dt 24:19, 22).

Some centuries later, the child Jesus was brought to the temple for the day of His presentation. The parents offered the priest a pair of turtledoves, the offering proscribed for a poor family. As He grew in wisdom, age, and grace, He never lost His love for the poor, His sensitivity for those who struggle, for the outcast and downtrodden, for the weary of heart. He yearns that we share the Father's life and love; His hope is that we would understand that this very gift of the Father is what gives us beauty and dignity. "The poor have good news preached to them" (Mt 11:5), was His response to the Baptist's messengers. The Gospel news is that their names are written on the palm of God's hands, inscribed on His heart. The last shall be first.

> Are not five sparrows sold for two pennies? And not one of them is forgotten before God. Why, even the hairs of your head are all numbered. Fear not; you are of more value than many sparrows (Lk 12:6-7).

NOTES

[1] As quoted by Andrew Louth, *The Wilderness of God* (Nashville: Abingdon Press, 1991), p. 29.

[2] St. Augustine, *The Confessions*, translated by Maria Boulding, O.S.B. (New York: Vintage Books, 1997), p. 222.

[3] Sheryl Frances Chen, "Cistercian Studies Quarterly," 2001, p. 306.

[4] The story on pages 26-28 originally appeared in *Liguori*, November 2002; it was later printed in *The Best Catholic Writing of 2004*, edited by Brian Doyle (Chicago: Loyola Press, 2004), pp. 203-205.

[5] The reflections on pages 34-37 first appeared as an article in *The Priest* magazine, September, 2003.

[6] T.S. Eliot, "Animula," *Selected Poems* (New York: Harcourt Brace, 1958), p. 101.

[7] Henri Nouwen, *Can You Drink the Cup?* (Notre Dame, IN: Ave Maria Press, 1996), p.83.

[8] Raymond Brown, *The Death of the Messiah* (New York: Doubleday, 1994), Vol. II, p. 1077.

[9] A Carthusian, *The Way of Silent Love* (Kalamazoo, MI: Cistercian Publications, 1993), p. 25.

[10] Ibid., p. 64.

[11] John Haughey, S.J., *The Conspiracy of God: The Holy Spirit in Men* (Garden City, NY: Doubleday, 1973), p. 11.

[12] Ronald Rolheiser, *The Shattered Lantern* (New York: Crossroads, 1994), p. 106.

[13] Kathleen Norris, *Amazing Grace: A Vocabulary of Faith* (New York: Riverhead Books, 1998), p. 106.

[14] Ram Dass, *Be Here Now* (New York: Crown Publishing Group, 1978), p.14.

[15] Henri Nouwen, *The Inner Voice of Love* (New York: Image Books, 1998), p. 31.

[16] José Marins y Equipo, *De Todas Las Razas y Naciones* (Que-

zon City, Philippines: Claretion Publications, 1998), p.78. Translation is my own.

¹⁷ Rachel Naomi Remen, M.D., *My Grandfather's Blessings* (New York: Riverhead Books, 2000), p. 38.

¹⁸ Catherine de Hueck Doherty, as quoted in *Magnificat,* July, 2004, Vol. 6, No. 5, p. 357.

¹⁹ Carson McCullers, *Reflections in a Golden Eye* (Boston: Mariner Books, 1941), p. 90.

²⁰· Raymond Brown, *The Death of the Messiah* (New York: Doubleday, 1994), Vol II, p. 1002.

²¹ *Maximus Confessor: Selected Writings (Classics of Western Spirituality)* (Mahwah, NJ: Paulist Press, 1985), p.34, no. 49.

²² St. John of the Cross, "The Dark Night," *The Collected Works of St. John of the Cross* (Washington, D.C.: ICS Publications, 1991), p. 382.

²³ Gerald C. May, M.D., *The Dark Night of the Soul* (San Francisco: Harper, 2003), p. 78.

²⁴ A Monk, *The Hermitage of the Heart* (Kalamazoo, MI: Cistercian Publications, 1977), p. 45.

²⁵ Susan Muto, *Pathways of Spiritual Living* (Petersham, MA: St. Bede's Publications, 1977), p. 45

²⁶ Anthony de Mello, *The Way to Love* (New York: Image Pocketbook Classics, Doubleday, 1992), p. 72.

²⁷ St. John of the Cross, *The Ascent of Mt. Carmel,* op. cit., Bk. 1, Ch. 13.

²⁸ Ray Hudson, *Moments Rightly Placed* (Seattle, WA: Epicenter Press, 1998).

²⁹ S.H. Hooke, "The Spirit Was Not Yet," *New Testament Studies,* 1963, Vol. 9, p. 378.

³⁰ Quoted by Pope John Paul II, *Letter to the Elderly* (Washington, D.C.: USCCB Press, 1999).

³¹ Quoted in *The Hermitage of the Heart,* op. cit., p. 8.

³² *Maximus Confessor,* op. cit., p. 156, no. 40.

³³ Ronald Rolheiser, op. cit., p. 180.

³⁴ St. Irenaeus of Lyons, *On the Apostolic Preaching* (Crestwood, NY: St. Vladimir's Seminary Press, 1997), p. 1.

³⁵ St. Augustine, op. cit., p. 222.

³⁶ St. Ignatius of Antioch, *Letter to the Romans,* quoted in "The

Liturgy of the Hours" (New York: Catholic Book Publishing Co., 1975), Vol. IV, p. 1490.

[37] Jim Wallis, *New York Times,* Dec. 28, 2003, Editorial Page.

[38] Ernst Benz, *The Eastern Orthodox Church* (Garden City, NY: Doubleday, 1963), p. 10 ff.

[39] Eamon Duffy, *The Stripping of the Altars* (New York: Yale Press, 1992), p. 112 ff.

[40] Georges Bernanos, *The Diary of a Country Priest* (New York: Carrol & Graf Publishers, 2004), p. 54.

[41] Albert Nolan, *Jesus Before Christianity* (Maryknoll, NY: Orbis Books, 2001), p. 122.

[42] Diadochus of Photice, *On Spiritual Perfection,* quoted in "The Liturgy of the Hours," op. cit., Vol. III, p. 101.

[43] Parts of this chapter first appeared in the liturgical journal, *Celebration,* November, 2004.

[44] James Carroll, *Wonder and Worship* (Paramus, NJ: Newman Press, 1970), p. 13.

[45] Eamon Duffy, "Faith of Our Fathers" (London: Continuum, 2004), p. 150.

[46] Dorotheus of Gaza, *Discources and Sayings* (Kalamazoo, MI: Cistercian Publications), 1977, p. 123.

[47] St. Thomas Aquinas, *Opusc. De Beatitudine, cap. II,* quoted in "The Inner Person" (Quebec, Canada: Maurice Zundel, Mediaspaul, 1996), p. 6.

[48] Kathleen Norris, op. cit., p. 273.

[49] Fyodor Dostoevsky, *The Brothers Karamazov* (New York: Farrar, Straus, and Giroux, 2002), p. 319.

[50] The story on pages 153-155 first appeared in *America,* November 2004.

[51] Henry Nouwen, *The Way of the Heart* (New York: Balantine Books, 1981), p. 20.

[52] Raymond Blakney, *Meister Eckhart* (New York: Harper Torchbooks, 1941), p. 123.

[53] Henri Nouwen, *The Inner Voice of Love* (New York: Image Books, 1998), p. 29.

[54] Antoninus Everson, *The Flight in the Desert,* quoted in "The Liturgy of the Hours," op. cit., Vol. I, p. 1667, emphasis added.

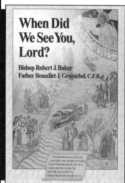